INTRODUCTION TO
EQUESTRIAN SPORTS

To Isabelle and Harry

INTRODUCTION TO
EQUESTRIAN
SPORTS

KATE LUXMOORE

LAND
LINKS

National Library of Australia Cataloguing-in-Publication entry

> Luxmoore, Kate.
> Introduction to equestrian sports.

> Bibliography.
> Includes index.
> ISBN 9780643094796 (pbk.).

> 1. Trail riding. 2. Show riding. 3. Eventing (Horsemanship).
> 4. Show jumping. 5. Dressage. 6. Horsemanship. 7. Horse sports.
> I. Title.

> 798.2

Published by and available from:
Landlinks Press
150 Oxford Street (PO Box 1139)
Collingwood VIC 3066
Australia

Telephone: +61 3 9662 7666
Local call: 1300 788 000 (Australia only)
Fax: +61 3 9662 7555
Email: publishing.sales@csiro.au
Web site: www.landlinks.com

Landlinks Press is an imprint of **CSIRO** PUBLISHING

Front cover: Showjumping (Julie Wilson Photography)

Back cover, left to right: Cross-country (OZ Equestrian Photography), dressage (OZ Equestrian Photography), showing (Julie Wilson Photography)

Set in Adobe Minion 11/13.5 and Adobe Helvetica Neue
Edited by Adrienne de Kretser, Righting Writing
Cover and text design by James Kelly
Typeset by Desktop Concepts P/L, Melbourne
Printed in Australia by BPA Print Group

The opinions, advice and information contained in this publication have not been provided at the request of any person but are offered solely to provide information.

While the information contained in this publication has been formulated with all due care the publisher, author and agents accept no responsibility for any person acting or relying on or upon any opinion, advice or information and disclaims all liability for any error, omission, defect or mis-statement (whether such error, omission, defect or mis-statement is caused by or arises from negligence or otherwise) or for any loss or other consequence that may arise from any person relying on anything in this publication.

Foreword

The world of equestrian sports can be confusing for new riders and their parents. There are so many different disciplines and events, so many rules to follow – both written and unwritten. We have all made mistakes – many a champion rider started out warming up in the wrong area or wearing the wrong gear.

There are many 'how to ride' books available. These are generally very useful for beginning riders but they don't usually talk about equestrian competitions in much detail. This book is different. It is a simple, easy-to-read guide for newcomers to equestrian sports, with all the information you need. It also offers handy tips to help you perform at your best. Who knows, it may be you competing for Australia one day!

Gillian Rolton OAM
Dual Olympic eventing team Gold Medallist (1992 Barcelona and 1996 Atlanta)
NCAS Level 3 coach and examiner
FEI International eventing judge and Advanced National dressage judge

Contents

Acknowledgments

I would like to thank the following people and organisations for their help and support in the preparation of this book.

Helen McMillan, Christine Peck and Tim Clarke for their tireless proofreading and content suggestions. Adrian McMillan, Jennifer Peck, Sally Ryan, Jason James, Travis Grieve, Kerry Edwards, Melton Saddlery and Mal Byrne Saddlery for their terrific photographs.

Gillian Rolton for lending her support to this book by providing the foreword.

I would also like to thank the Equestrian Federation of Australia, the Pony Club Association of Victoria and the Horse Riding Clubs Association of Victoria, for the use of their association rules as references in writing this book.

My Mum, my Dad and my sister Emma for all their support, not only on this project but throughout my riding career, especially all the early mornings driving to competitions!

Finally my wonderful husband Rohan, for his contributions to this book and for putting up with me tapping on the computer into the wee small hours for weeks on end!

About the author

Kate Luxmoore grew up in the Victorian high country town of Rawson and started riding at the age of five. She spent every free moment riding her pony Goldie through the bush. The family moved to Geelong when Kate was in her early teens and it was there she commenced her competitive riding career. She dabbled in all the equestrian disciplines, with success, before focusing her attention on dressage.

Kate has been very successful in the dressage arena, reaching Grand Prix level with her horses Timbertop and Jilba Ben. Kate is also an NCAS-accredited riding instructor, although she is not currently teaching due to the demands of a young family and full-time work as an IT project manager.

Kate and her husband Rohan, who is an advanced level eventing rider, live with their two children Isabelle and Harry on a property on the outskirts of Melbourne.

The author with her Grand Prix Champion horse Timbertop.

1
Introduction

Buying a horse seemed like a good idea at the time, so why are you sitting in your car on Sunday at 5 am? Nobody told you that you would be towing a horse float to a town you've never heard of, for a competition which you can't understand.

Horses are much more than just a hobby. They are a lifestyle and an addiction. Horse riding is one of the few sports where age is no barrier, even at the elite level – 70-year-old Lorna Johnstone rode at the 1972 Olympics. The social and family friendly atmosphere is as much a drawcard as the competition itself.

Many social riders progress to competition riding, but that step into the competition arena can be daunting. *Introduction to Equestrian Sports* is not a 'how to ride' book – it is a book that will help parents and riders who are new to the world of equestrian sports. It explains different types of competitions and describes the basic rules and objectives of each. It is a guide to training and equipment and offers other handy hints to help you make a successful move to equestrian competition.

With this knowledge under your belt, I hope your move into the competition arena will be both successful and enjoyable.

Disciplines

There are a number of different disciplines that fall under the banner of equestrian sports. This book covers the four that are most common in Australia.

- **Hacking/showing:** Hacking/showing competitions focus on the beauty and elegance of horses and riders. They are a wonderful way to start a competitive equestrian career, particularly for junior riders.

- **Dressage:** Dressage is the equestrian world's equivalent to ballet or gymnastics. Horses and riders perform a series of complex and difficult movements which look like a beautiful and effortless dance.
- **Eventing/horse trials:** Eventing/horse trials are the triathlon of the equestrian world and the discipline of choice for adrenaline junkies as they combine dressage, cross-country jumping and showjumping. An eventing horse and rider need elegance, technique and bravery to win the blue ribbon.
- **Showjumping:** Showjumping requires a horse and rider to be careful yet brave to successfully clear a series of jumps which fall down with just a light touch of a hoof. Showjumping is measured objectively – it is the only discipline where the subjective opinion of a judge has no bearing on results.

2

Hacking/showing

Hacking/showing is not an Olympic sport and is usually not competed at an international level, although there are now a number of international video competitions. Hacking classes are held at horse shows conducted by various organisations.

Hacking originated in England as a key component of agricultural shows. At these shows, competitors would display animals such as cattle and horses that they had bred. Prizes were presented to the animals with the best conformation (structural proportions) and qualities that were most important to their breed, e.g. dairy cows were selected on conformation and milk production. Hacking began as a way to show off a horse's quality, and grew from there. Horse shows are no longer just part of an agricultural show – they are often an event in their own right. Showing is best described as a beauty pageant for horses. Horses still have to perform certain movements correctly, but basically a horse is judged on its overall beauty – a combination of its presentation, conformation and movement. There are also classes where a rider is judged on their ability to ride and the horse's beauty is not taken into account, and other classes which judge the combination of horse and rider.

There are several different types of horse shows and many different classes at the shows themselves.

Types of classes
Types and quantities of hacking classes vary enormously between horse shows but can generally be divided into six categories:

- horse classes
- rider classes
- turnout and smartest-on-parade classes
- novice and consolation classes
- fun/topsy classes
- championships.

Horse classes

So that similar horses are grouped together, horse classes are restricted by a horse's height and sometimes by its sex and age. Horses are sorted into four basic height groups:

- small ponies – under 12.2hh
- large ponies – from 12.2hh but under 14hh
- galloways – from 14hh but under 15hh
- hacks – 15hh and over.

> **TIP:** hh stands for 'hands high'. Hands are the most common unit for measuring a horse. One hand = 4 inches (9 cm), so a measurement of 12.3hh = (12 × 4 inches) + 3 inches= 51 inches (115 cm). Some horses are measured down to the fraction of an inch such as 12.1¾hh.

> **TIP:** The term 'hack' can be very confusing. A horse over 15hh is known as a hack, but the word can also refer to any horse that is ridden. This comes from the term 'to hack out', which means to go for a ride. Some horse shows include classes such as:
>
> - ridden pony hack 13hh but not exceeding 13.2hh.
>
> You can ignore the word 'hack', as it has no meaning in defining the class.

The height of a horse is measured from the ground to the top of the horse's wither, which is the highest point on the horse's back immediately behind where its neck joins its body. A horse must be measured while standing on level ground, using a measuring stick. Most show organisers have a measuring stick and will measure your horse to see which class you should be competing in, if you are unsure of your horse's height. A horse's height is always taken as the height without shoes. Having said that, you do not need to remove a horse's shoes to measure it – the measurer will calculate an allowance for the shoes.

Horses are grouped into five basic categories for sex:

- stallions – uncastrated male horses 4 yrs and over
- colts – uncastrated male horses under 4 yrs of age
- geldings – castrated male horses of any age
- mares – female horses 4 yrs and over
- fillies – female horses under 4 yrs.

Led classes

In a led class the horse wears only a bridle and does not have a rider. Horses in this type of class are judged primarily on their conformation and movement. A led class will be described in a manner similar to this:

- led hack 15hh but not exceeding 15.2hh *or*
- led mare 15hh but not exceeding 15.2hh.

'Conformation' basically means the correctness of its physique, a very complex area. However, there are certain physical characteristics that a judge will look for in a led class, such as:

- the horse's proportions (e.g. length of neck, length of body)
- the correctness of the horse's legs (e.g. straightness)
- the shape and angles of the horse's hoofs
- the horse's presentation (e.g. quality and cleanliness of coat)
- the horse's movement (e.g. whether the horse takes correct even steps).

A horse with correct conformation and movement is considered an ideal riding horse, as its movement will be more comfortable for the rider and the horse is less likely to injure itself. For example, a horse with crooked legs is considered more likely to strain its legs than a horse with straight legs.

Some judges penalise a horse that has faults caused by injury, such as scars, although other judges don't penalise such faults as they are considered to be acquired not inherent faults.

Key judging criteria

Very important to judging

- Conformation
- Movement.

Moderately important

- Horse's presentation
- Horse's behaviour/temperament/manners.

Beautiful led hack with a champion sash. Although the handler's attire is not judged in this class you should still be well presented as a mark of respect to the judge. Photo: Julie Wilson Photography

Not important
- Handler's presentation, although you should always be neat and tidy.

Ridden classes

In a ridden class the horse is judged primarily on its conformation, movement and education (training). A ridden class will be described in a manner similar to:

- ridden hack 15hh but not exceeding 15.2hh *or*
- ridden mare 15hh but not exceeding 15.2hh *or*
- ridden pony 12hh but not exceeding 12.2hh, must be ridden by a child under 10 yrs.

Although some ridden classes specify the age of the rider, the rider is not judged. The judge will assess the horse's education on criteria such as the following:

- whether the horse is well behaved, i.e. does as the rider asks
- whether the horse works on the bit, i.e. its head and neck are in correct position and it responds correctly to the rider's signals
- whether the horse canters correctly on each leg, i.e. uses a left lead in a left circle and a right lead in a right circle.

TIP: Knowing which leg a horse is cantering on is important. For example, when cantering on the right lead a horse's legs must hit the ground in the following sequence: left hind leg, right hind and left fore together, right fore, then a moment of suspension when all four legs are off the ground. If you watch a horse's front legs you will see that one leg goes farther forward than the other front leg. The leg that goes farther forward is the lead.

Many beginner riders are frustrated when a competitor whose horse has misbehaved is placed higher in the class. The judge's decision is based on the overall criteria rather than a single element. For example, a judge weighs a mistake against a horse's conformation and movement – if the mistake is slight and the conformation and movement are excellent, the horse may be placed high in the results. A rider whose horse has poorer conformation and movement can't afford any mistakes if they want to win.

Key judging criteria
Very important to judging
- Horse's education
- Horse's behaviour
- Conformation
- Movement.

Moderately important
- Horse's presentation
- Rider's presentation.

TIP: 'Hunter hack' classes are relatively new in Australia and are becoming increasingly popular. A hunter hack class is the same as a normal ridden class except for the following:

- the judge will be looking for a heavier type of horse
- the horse's bridle should not be decorated (beginner riders need not worry too much, use your normal bridle)
- the horse may be asked to gallop
- the horse will not be asked to jump
- the rider should not wear ribbons in their hair.

This should not be confused with a 'working hunter' class where the horse will be asked to jump and will be judged on its suitability as a hunter horse, to ride with hounds when fox hunting.

Beautifully presented horse victorious in a ridden horse class. Photo: Julie Wilson Photography

Rider classes

In a rider class, the rider is judged, not the horse. The rider will be judged on how well they ride.

Riders are grouped by age, and some big shows may have separate classes for males and females. A show program lists a rider class in a manner similar to:

- rider 10 yrs and over but under 12 yrs *or*
- lady rider 18 yrs and over.

Judging a rider's ability is relatively subjective, but all judges look for a rider who is both 'attractive' and 'effective'. 'Attractive' doesn't mean a beautiful or handsome person – it refers to the attractiveness of the rider's technique. Ideally, the rider should make the quite physical task of riding a horse look effortless.

Pony competing in a hunter hack class. In a hunter hack class the bridle should be plain and there should be no ribbons or decorations in the rider's hair. Jackets, ties and vests should be conservative and simple and not too colourful. At bigger shows, horses and riders are required to wear a number. You will need to provide your own number-holder. Photo: Julie Wilson Photography

A judge will be looking for qualities such as:

- a rider who sits quite still
- a rider whose hands are quite still
- a rider who sits up straight
- a rider who rises on the correct diagonal
- a rider whose legs stay still and whose heels stay down.

TIP: Knowing which diagonal you are rising on is important. A horse can carry a rider's weight better and balance correctly if the rider rises on the correct diagonal. With a rising trot a rider will be in the 'up' position for one beat of the trot and the 'down' position for the other beat. When riding on a circle a rider must be in the up position when the horse's outside foreleg is off the ground. If there is a change of direction (such as riding a figure eight) the rider must also change diagonals – sit for two trot beats then start rising again.

Although the horse is not judged, its behaviour is an indication of how 'effective' the rider is, e.g. a rider who sits very still but who can't make the horse canter on the correct leg may be an attractive rider but not an effective one. The judge has to balance the rider's attractiveness and effectiveness. A rider on a misbehaving horse may win a rider class if the judge decides that they rode the horse very effectively.

Key judging criteria
Very important to judging
- Rider's attractiveness as a rider
- Rider's effectiveness
- A rider who makes riding look effortless.

Moderately important
- Horse's education/behaviour (as this reflects on the rider's effectiveness)
- Rider's presentation
- Horse's presentation.

Not important
- Horse's movement
- Horse's conformation.

Turnout and smartest-on-parade classes
Many competitors consider that a turnout or smartest-on-parade class is the pinnacle of showing. One of the most famous turnout classes is the Garryowen, held each year at the Royal Melbourne Show.

In a turnout class the qualities of horse and rider are judged together. The horse/rider combination is also judged on the quality and correctness of their riding outfit and saddlery.

At royal shows, rider-of-the-year shows and large agricultural shows, turnout classes may have multiple judges, each awarding points for a certain aspect. For example, one may judge the rider's clothes, while another judges the horse's workout and conformation. In these elite turnout classes the judging process may take hours as each competitor is examined in minute detail. At smaller shows, the inspection is less intensive but the judge still gives competitors a very close inspection. Competitors also perform a workout as part of the judging criteria.

In a smartest-on-parade competition riders will be judged on the circle only as they walk, trot and canter as a group around the judge. Prizes are awarded to the horse and rider combinations who most appeal to the judge from a distance. Competitors are not required to do individual workouts.

Although a certain standard of dress is required in all equestrian competitions, a turnout class takes this to another level. In a turnout class at a big show (open horse shows and bigger) the judge will look for qualities such as:

- a hand-picked (hand-sewn) jacket and jodhpurs
- 12 stitches to each inch (2.25 cm) of sewing on the horse's bridle
- leather covers over the buttons at the front of the saddle
- the neatness of the horse's plaits
- the shine of the horse's coat.

The judge must weigh up all the criteria, but it is not unknown for a class to be won because the soles of that rider's boots were cleaner than another's!

At smaller shows the judge focuses on the cleanliness and neatness of the horse and rider rather than the quality of their dress or equipment. At some shows this type of class is listed as a 'Best-presented' event, with competitors' saddlery and equipment judged solely on presentation rather than quality.

Key judging criteria
Very important to judging
- Rider's attractiveness as a rider
- Rider's effectiveness
- Horse's education (as this reflects on the rider's effectiveness)
- Rider's presentation, especially the quality of the dress
- Horse's presentation
- Quality and presentation of saddlery
- Horse's movement
- Horse's conformation
- Horse's manners/temperament.

> TIP: Turnout classes can be very expensive. Many riders keep a separate riding outfit, saddle and bridle just for turnout classes. This is a waste of time for a beginner, whose money is better spent on riding lessons. Beginner riders should present themselves in a clean and tidy fashion in turnout classes only at smaller shows, and not bother buying all the gear required to win a turnout class at bigger shows. At smaller shows a turnout class is judged more on the cleanliness of horse and equipment rather than on quality.

Novice and consolation classes
Novice classes
Most shows run novice classes designed for beginner riders and/or beginner horses. A novice is a competitor who has not won a first place in the novice class they are entering.

A novice class will be described in the program in a manner similar to:

- novice ridden hack 15hh but not exceeding 15.2hh *or*
- novice led hack 15hh but not exceeding 15.2hh *or*

- novice ridden pony 12hh but not exceeding 12.2hh, must be ridden by a child under 10 yrs.

All classes (horse, rider and turnout) can be run in a novice format. This restricts the number of competitors and gives beginners an opportunity to compete against those of a similar standard. Riders can compete in both the novice and the normal (open) class at the same show, as they are usually run one after the other. Once a rider has won a novice or an open class, they can no longer compete in that type of novice class.

Novice classes can be quite confusing. For example, a rider can win a novice ridden class such as 'novice ridden hack 15hh but not exceeding 15.2hh' but still be eligible to compete in a novice rider class such as 'novice rider 10 yrs but under 12 yrs'. In other words, you may be a novice rider but your horse may not be a novice horse. If you buy a horse that has done some showing, the horse may not be allowed to compete in a novice class if it won with the previous owner. However, you may still compete in your novice rider class.

Show organisers may have special rules regarding novice classes. Make sure you read the program carefully.

Eligibility for a novice class is purely an honour system. If a rider won a class at one show they are expected not to compete in the novice class at a different show. Other riders deserve a chance.

> **TIP:** If you win a novice class it only means you are no longer a novice for that type of show and any shows below that level. For example, if you win your novice class at an open horse show, you can still go in the novice class at an agricultural show. Open horse shows and open gymkhanas are considered to be on the same level regarding eligibility for novice classes.

Consolation classes

Consolation classes were designed to make sure no one went home without a ribbon. They are no longer held as often as they used to be. These classes are usually the last of the day and are generally only open to competitors who haven't won a ribbon in that type of class that day. A class such as 'consolation rider under 12 yrs' is for riders who haven't won a ribbon in any of the rider classes that day. They are very good classes, especially for children. The program will specify the rules.

Fun/topsy classes

These are classes designed specifically for very young and beginner children. As their name suggests, the classes are meant to be fun. A fun ring may have classes such as:

- pony with the longest tail
- fluffiest pony

Dressed and ready to go in the topsy ring.

- neatest rider
- pony most like its owner.

These rings often have dress-up classes and generally hand out lots of ribbons. It is not unusual for a judge to give a ribbon to everyone in the class, with lots of equal placings!

As with the novice classes, competing in the fun ring is essentially an honour system and should not be abused by riders who are above this level.

> **TIP:** Fun rings are a wonderful introduction to showing for children. Everyone will go home with a bag of ribbons and a good judge will share the first-place ribbons around.

Championships

Championships are generally awarded for led, ridden and rider classes. A championship will judge the winners from classes such as:

- rider 10 yrs and under 12 yrs
- rider 12 yrs and under 14 yrs
- rider 14 yrs and under 16 yrs.

Winners will compete for 'champion rider 10 yrs and under 16 yrs'. Once the championship ribbon has been awarded, the competitor who received the second-place ribbon to the champion can enter the ring to compete for reserve (runner-up) champion.

The program will specify who is eligible to compete for the various championships. For example, the program usually shows:

- champion rider 10 yrs and under 16 yrs (winners from classes 6, 8 and 9).

Supreme championships are awarded at some shows. These are 'champion of champions' classes. Most shows include:

- supreme champion led exhibit
- supreme champion ridden exhibit
- supreme champion rider.

The champions from each ring compete for these awards. For example, the champion ridden pony, champion ridden galloway and champion ridden hack will compete for supreme champion ridden exhibit. The program will specify who is eligible to compete for supreme champion.

Types of horse shows

Closed and novice gymkhanas

These shows are usually quite small and generally run by pony or riding clubs. As their name suggests, the shows are not open to all competitors. Closed gymkhanas may be restricted to members of the pony club association or to members of an individual pony club. Novice gymkhanas are restricted to novice riders/horses. The gymkhanas usually involve the following:

- there are a small number of classes, usually including 'fun rings', with classes restricted to young riders and beginners
- they are run on a single day
- they are run under the rules of the Equestrian Federation of Australia (EFA), although shows restricted to pony or riding club members may use the rules of their own association
- horses and riders *do not* need to be registered with the EFA but may need to be a member of the pony or riding club association to compete at their shows
- stallions and colts are *not* usually allowed to compete
- horse/rider may need to qualify for a pony club gymkhana by attending a certain number of pony club meets (rallies)
- prizes won at closed gymkhanas are not accepted as qualifications for horse/rider of the year and royal shows.

Open gymkhanas

These shows vary enormously in size but are in general a smaller version of an open horse show. They are generally run by the same types of associations that run open horse shows. They usually involve the following:

- there are a medium number of classes, usually including 'fun rings', with classes restricted to young riders and beginners
- they are run over one day
- they are normally run under EFA rules
- horses and riders *do not* need to be registered with the EFA or any specific society unless competing in a breed class
- horse/rider *do not* need to qualify for the event they are entering
- stallions and colts are *not* usually allowed to compete
- prizes won at gymkhanas are *not* accepted as qualifications for horse/rider of the year and royal shows.

Open horse shows

These shows vary enormously in size and can be run by a variety of organisations. The shows are usually run by pony or riding clubs as a fundraiser but they are also run by schools, fire brigades and any other organisation you can imagine. These shows are just for horses – they rarely have any of the side shows found at agricultural shows. Usually, they involve the following:

- there are a medium number of classes (breed classes are rare at these shows)
- they are run over one to three days generally
- they are normally run under EFA rules
- horses and riders *do not* need to be registered with the EFA or any specific society unless competing in a breed class
- horse/rider *do not* need to qualify for the event they are entering
- stallions and colts are *not* usually allowed to compete
- prizes won at some larger horse shows are accepted as qualifications for horse/ rider of the year and royal shows.

Breed shows

Breed shows are run by specific breed associations and are restricted to horses or ponies registered with that particular breed. The Arabian horse, Riding pony and Warmblood societies are a few of the associations which run breed shows. They usually require both horse and owner to be registered with the breed association. Most breed associations recognise a horse's registration for life, but an owner generally has to renew membership each year. If you purchase a horse which is registered with a breed association, check with that association whether you too need to be registered in order to compete in its breed show. Usually with breed shows:

- there are a medium number of classes, often with large numbers of led classes dedicated to young and breeding stock
- they are run over one day
- they are run under EFA rules
- horses and owners must be registered with the breed association running the show
- horse/rider sometimes (not always) need to qualify for the event they are entering at very big breed shows
- stallions and colts are usually allowed to compete. Breed shows place a high importance on breeding stock and are an opportunity to showcase breed animals
- prizes won at breed shows are accepted as qualifications for breed classes at royal shows.

Agricultural shows

These shows are usually run by the agricultural society in various country towns. Their size varies enormously. Large shows may involve the same variety of animals as royal shows, while others may be limited to just a few animal types. Usually with agricultural shows:

- there are a medium number of classes (smaller agricultural shows may not have any breed classes)
- they are run over one to three days
- they are run under the rules of the state's agricultural society association
- horses and riders do not need to be registered with the EFA or any specific society unless competing in a breed class
- horse/rider *do not* need to qualify for the event they are entering
- prizes won at agricultural shows are accepted as qualifications for horse/rider of the year and royal shows.

Horse/rider of the year shows

Horses and riders must win their state horse/rider of the year show to qualify for the national show, and are therefore representing their state at the national final. Competitors are eligible to enter their state horse/rider of the year show if they have won at various qualifying events during the previous year. These shows usually involve the following:

- there are a very limited number of classes
- they are run over one to two days
- they are run under EFA rules

The grand parade at a royal show. Photo: Julie Wilson Photography

- horses and riders may need to be registered with the EFA
- horse/rider must qualify for the event they are entering.

Many riders consider these shows to be the highest level of competition in the sport of hacking.

Royal shows

These horse shows are part of the royal agricultural shows held annually in each Australian capital city and a selection of rural cities. Horses are only one of the many types of animals and produce on display at these events. Royal shows usually involve the following:

- there are a large number of classes
- they are run over one to two weeks
- they are run under the rules of the state's agricultural society association
- horses and riders do not need to be registered with the EFA or any specific society unless competing in a breed class
- horse/rider must qualify for the event they are entering.

Many riders also consider royal shows to be the highest level of competition in the sport of hacking.

Ground rules

Where to park

When you arrive you may be directed to park in a particular area. If you aren't, it is best to find out which ring you will be competing in and then, if possible, park near your ring so that you can keep an eye on what is going on. This also gives your support crew (if you're lucky enough to have one) a good viewing position.

If you are riding to the show you will need somewhere to tie your horse. Find out beforehand whether the ground has yards or a tie-up area, and make sure you get there *very* early to reserve your spot.

What to wear

Neat and tidy is the key. When starting out it is easy to get overwhelmed with dress requirements. You don't need to have everything on day 1 – a school jumper and tie make an excellent outfit if you are just starting in the show ring. You can buy the required outfits over time. Make sure that your purchases are in line with the dress code, for example there is no point spending money on lovely black-top boots for a junior rider if black-top boots aren't allowed in the ring. Full details of saddlery and dress guidelines for the show ring can be found in the showing rulebook on the EFA website (see Further reading).

As a general rule the dress code is as follows.

Riders under 16 yrs
- Fawn, banana or similar colour jodhpurs (not white)
- Shirt, usually white (always white or pale cream for turnout) but many riders are being adventurous with their colours these days
- Tie, plain straight tiepin and cufflinks
- Riding jacket, traditionally blue/grey/brown but nearly any colour goes if you're brave enough to try. Traditional colours must be worn in turnout classes. Juniors should not wear black jackets
- Riding vest under the jacket, with the edge of the vest visible along the jacket's lapel
- Short brown elastic-sided boots which *must* have a flat/non-grip sole. Workboots with a grip sole are not acceptable
- Fawn or similar coloured gloves for turnout, with leather palms and string backs. You can wear these for all classes but it is a better idea to wear dark gloves for other classes so that your fawn ones stay clean
- Australian Standards approved helmet, preferably velvet covered, in a colour to match your riding jacket
- Hacking cane for rider and turnout/smartest-on-parade classes.

Correct junior attire for a rider class. The rosette is tied to the rider's arm, indicating that this is a rider class. In a horse class the rosette is attached to the horse's bridle. Photo: Julie Wilson Photography

Riders 16 yrs and over

Same guidelines as for riders under 16 except for the following.

- Long black leather or good-quality synthetic boots (top boots) may be worn except in turnout classes, smartest-on-parade and rider classes where a rider must be 18 before they can wear top boots. Top boots are not compulsory. Short boots can be worn by riders of any age and are often worn by adults riding ponies.

Riders over 18 in turnout classes
- Dark coloured riding jacket (black, navy or charcoal)
- Fawn breeches
- Long white shirt and white stock with a stockpin and cufflinks
- Black leather top boots

- Fawn gloves with leather palms and string backs
- Bowler hat, unless the organising committee specifies that an Australian Standards approved helmet must be worn
- Hacking cane.

Pony club, riding club and schools classes
- Full pony/riding/school club uniform, including an Australian Standards approved helmet
- Pony club associations have their own rules on whether riders over 18 can wear long leather boots – check the rule book
- Pony/riding club grading card
- Pony club riders must wear a medical armband (either arm) over their clothing.

When you are starting out the following is acceptable in all classes except pony/riding club and school competitions, where a uniform must be worn.

- Clean jodhpurs, preferably fawn, banana or similar
- White shirt
- Simple tie
- V-neck jumper or similar (school jumper or pony club jumper can be worn in any class)
- Australian Standards approved helmet
- Short elastic-sided boots
- Plain dark leather gloves.

TIP: How you present yourself is more important than whether you have the correct equipment.

- Your hair must be very neat. If you have long hair, make sure it is in a bun or plait and covered with a hairnet.
- Your clothes must be very clean. Wear a tracksuit over your jodhpurs between classes to keep them clean.
- Your shoes must be very polished. Take them off between classes to keep them clean.
- Your tie and collar must be straight and your collar must sit flat. A tiepin is a good idea.
- Make sure that your jodhpurs don't ride up when you are wearing short boots so that your socks are showing. Use jodhpur clips or sew elastic inside your jodhpurs like a stirrup that passes under your foot inside your boot.

The term jodhpurs and breeches are sometimes used interchangeably to describe riding pants but there are important differences between them. Jodhpurs are riding pants that are designed to be worn with short riding boots. They extend beyond your ankle so that you can pull them over the top of the short boots. In junior turnout classes, you can wear jodhpurs with a small cuff and zip at the bottom of the leg. Breeches are short riding pants down to your shin. They fasten above your ankle with a Velcro attachment and are designed to be used with top boots. The breeches are less bulky around your ankles and so are more comfortable than jodhpurs if you are wearing top boots. You can wear jodhpurs with top boots, but you can never wear breeches with short boots.

Equipment

A dressage/show or turnout saddle should be used in the show ring. Ideally the saddle should be made of brown leather with a matching leather girth for turnout classes. If you are starting out, a synthetic saddle is fine in most classes but it will be frowned upon in turnout classes. Some riders use black saddles in the show ring to colour-coordinate better with black or grey horses – matching your saddle colour to your horse is definitely a luxury. If you want to show and you can only afford one saddle, choose brown. Synthetic girths are acceptable in all but turnout classes and should be either the same colour as the saddle or made of white webbing material.

Your stirrup leathers should be the same colour as your saddle and be stitched down either side for turnout classes. Stainless steel stirrup irons are used with white rubber inserts for all classes except turnouts, where knife-edge stirrups are correct. Knife-edge stirrups have a slightly rough surface on which your foot rests, and they have no rubber inserts.

Your bridle must *always* be the same colour as your saddle. In all classes except for turnout and hunter horse classes, browbands decorated with coloured ribbons are the current fashion. In turnout and hunter classes, browbands must be plain leather without decoration. Show bridles should have a cavesson noseband (see Chapter 7). The noseband can be raised or flat for all classes except turnouts, which require a flat noseband. A flat noseband is made of a single thickness of leather and is only stitched at the attaching points. A raised noseband is made by stitching two pieces of leather together along their entire length, giving a raised and slightly curved appearance.

> **TIP:** When you oil brown leather the colour will darken. If you are buying a new bridle to match your brown saddle make sure you choose one that is a shade or two lighter than the saddle, as it will match after you oil it. A saddlery store will help you choose the right shade of leather to get the best match.

Except in pony/riding club rings, which require rectangular club saddle cloths, use sheepskin saddle cloths shaped to fit around the saddle. These are known as numnahs. Numnahs can be purchased off the shelf but are often made to fit a specific saddle, as the numnah should exactly mirror the saddle. A variation is the half-pad, which is becoming increasingly popular. The half-pad is a shaped sheepskin saddle cloth that sits directly under the saddle but does not extend down the horse's side under the saddle flaps.

> **TIP:** If you want to do turnout classes but can't afford both an ordinary and a turnout set of saddlery, your turnout saddlery is more than acceptable in all your other classes. Professional riders have two saddlery kits primarily to maintain the pristine condition of their turnout equipment.

> **TIP:** If you have a turnout bridle with a plain browband but would like something a bit snazzier for the other classes, purchase a separate ribbon-covered browband and swap it onto your bridle after the turnout class.

Where to warm up

At smaller shows you are often allowed to warm up in the ring before judging commences. You *must* check with the organisers (or people selling tickets for the classes) to see if it's allowed before you ride in the rings. It is very good to ride in the ring as it will let your horse get used to the atmosphere and any scary decorations (such as flags) that may be around.

Once the first class has started you won't be allowed in the ring except when competing. This can make warming up between classes difficult at small grounds, but there is usually a small area to ride in. These areas can get very busy, so it is best to have a good ride early in the morning so that your horse will only need a little warm-up before each class.

At bigger competitions the area where you can warm up, and sometimes even the times you are allowed to practise, will be specified in the program.

> **TIP:** When hacking/showing, you can share a horse on the day of the competition. Several different riders may even use the same horse in different rider classes!

Riding in the show ring

Most classes follow much the same format. All horses eligible for a particular class enter the ring together and the gatekeeper or steward (who assists the judge with organisation of the ring) collects an entry ticket from each competitor. Entries may have to be made in advance at larger shows. If so, horses may be issued with a number that will be checked by the gatekeeper or steward.

The steward will ask competitors to circle around the judge as a group. In led classes, horses will only be asked to walk and maybe trot as a group (horses are never asked to canter in a led class). In most classes under saddle (classes where the horse is ridden) the horses will be asked to walk, trot and canter on the circle. Give yourself some space – never ride closer than at least one horse's body length behind another horse. Try to find a spot on the circle which is not crowded and keep towards the outside of the ring without getting hidden behind other competitors. Whatever you do, don't make a small circle close to the judge to make sure they see you – they don't appreciate being crowded!

The judge then asks the steward to 'call in' the riders they have selected from the group. The steward usually points and asks for the horse of a particular colour, for example 'the grey horse'. If you are chosen, you line up in the centre of the circle in the order the judge called. The judge usually calls the horses in the order they prefer, favourite horse first. The judge will call in a few more horses than they have ribbons to award. For example, if there are ribbons to fourth place the judge usually calls in six or seven horses (if they are intending to hold a workout). When the judge has called in all the competitors they require they usually say something along the lines of 'thank you riders'. If you weren't chosen, this is the signal to leave the arena.

The group of horses that was called in is referred to as the 'line-up'. The judge will look at the horses in the line-up and compare them side-by-side. They generally approach each rider and assess the horse by walking around it.

You may be asked to do a workout, a series of movements that competitors complete individually, such as:

- Walk out, trot a figure eight, canter a figure eight, halt and walk back to the judge.

You can ask the judge to repeat the workout requirements if you are unsure.

The judge will tell you what the workout is just before you have to do it. At very big shows where the workout is more complex, you will be given the workout to learn ahead of time. A workout generally consists of walk and trot (for led classes) and walk, trot and canter for ridden classes. Some classes with very small ponies and young riders may not be asked to canter.

One of the most telltale signs differentiating experienced and beginner show riders is their ability to effectively utilise the available space for their workout. Unlike the dressage arena, the show ring does not have any specific markers to which you perform your workout. You must use your skill to position your workout effectively. The most common mistake of novice riders is when they are asked to perform a figure eight movement. When riding a figure eight, the two circles should meet in the centre to form a straight line, giving the impression of two circles squashed together in the middle (see Figs 2.1 and 2.2). Novice riders tend to create a figure eight that looks like the number 8. This is not correct for the show ring. The other mistake novice riders make is to lose their bearings and overlap the circles. To avoid both these problems, choose a marker in the ring before riding your workout.

While in the line-up, identify an object in the centre of the ring fence where you will be doing your workout. It can be a particular float or maybe a rubbish bin

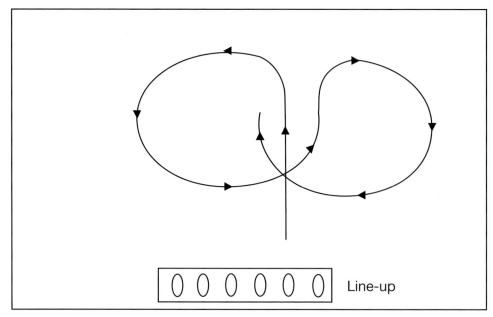

Figure 2.1: The incorrect way to ride a figure eight, overlapping circles with no central marker. The workout is also skewed to one side of the ring. You do not have to start your workout from your position in the line-up. If you are at the end of the line-up, walk to the centre of the ring before starting your workout.

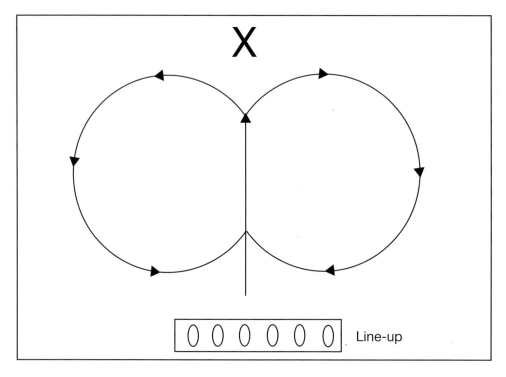

Figure 2.2: The correct way to ride a figure eight in the show ring, two circles squashed together with a straight line through the middle. X indicates your chosen marker.

– anything will do as long as it's very obvious. *Don't* choose one of the fence posts around the ring, as they all look the same when you are doing your workout. If the workout requires you to perform a figure eight, when it's your turn walk out from the line-up and over to the starting-point in line with your marker. As you ride your figure eight, subtly look to your marker to maintain your central position in the ring. *Don't* turn your head obviously to watch your marker while you ride the circle.

If you are given a workout where you are required to do a single circle, such as:

- walk out, trot a circle, canter a circle and return to the judge

don't squish your workout into one corner. For this type of workout, position your circle in the middle of the ring and ride right out to the ring fence. If you practise identifying markers and riding workouts at home, you will give a much better workout performance on show day.

> **TIP:** Always remain quiet in the line-up. Only speak when the judge or steward asks you a question, and don't chat to the other riders. If your horse won't stand quietly in the line-up, walk it in small circles behind the line-up until it is your turn with the judge. Be careful not to get in the way of riders completing their workout.

After the workout, the judge may rearrange the order of competitors. If so, they will ask you to bring your horses out of the line-up in the new order, and create a new line-up. The judge will then present the ribbons; the steward will write down the name of the horse and rider to give to the commentators.

After *all* the ribbons have been presented, horses leave the arena in the order in which the ribbons were presented.

> **TIP:** As the ribbons are being presented you may speak to congratulate your fellow competitors.

> **TIP:** Always stay in the order that you were awarded ribbons when you leave the arena. It is bad manners to overtake anyone.

Programs and entries

All shows provide a program of:

- the events they are running
- which events are in which ring
- what time the rings start (usually a time is given only for the start of the ring, the events are then simply run in order of the program with a lunch break)
- the price for each class

- sometimes the name of the judge in each ring.

Your local saddlery should have a copy of the program or you can contact the show organisers. Shows are often advertised in country/rural newspapers with the phone number of a person who can send you a program.

Smaller shows take entries on the day – you buy tickets from the organisers when you arrive. Tickets can usually be used in any event; you simply hand one to the steward when you enter a class.

At bigger shows you may have to decide beforehand which classes you wish to enter and send your entries to the organisers. The show program will state the closing date for entries – your entries must arrive by that date. Some big shows still allow you to enter on the day but will charge double the normal entry price for the privilege!

> **TIP:** Formerly, all shows ran each class only once, for example there would be one rider class for under 10 yrs. Recently it has become popular to run shows known as three-ring circuses. These shows have three main rings with each class being run three times – the class for riders under 10 yrs is run once in each ring. This means you can go in your riding class three times with three different judges. It gives everyone a better chance of winning a ribbon but it can also make quite an expensive day.
>
> Check the program to see if the classes are repeated in each ring, just in a different order. If they do this it is a three-ring circus show.

Arenas and classes

The size and quality of the riding arenas (rings) vary dramatically. A ring is a designated area where a class is judged, usually marked off by a rope with a single entrance. At some shows (where rope is in short supply) the arena may be roped off on only two sides and you have to estimate the other two sides.

There is no specific size for a show ring. Often, space is at a premium and you will be riding in a very small area.

The ring number is usually displayed on the gate or on a sign in the middle of the ring. If the ring isn't marked, the organisers will have a map that shows which ring is which.

If you are very lucky, the show will have a sign in the middle of each ring showing which class number is currently being judged. This doesn't happen often, so you must keep a close eye on the ring to know when your class is starting. Judges work very quickly, so make sure you are paying attention and don't be late! The start time for each class is not specified at a show, unlike dressage. The start time is specified for the ring, and classes simply run in order from that time. How long each class takes depends entirely on the number of competitors. Watch your ring closely and cross each class off your program as it is completed to help you keep track of where judges are up to.

> **TIP:** The type of ribbon and where it is being tied can help you determine what class a ring is up to. Sashes are wide ribbons with tassels on each end, awarded in turnout classes and for championships. Champion sashes are usually red/white/blue, while the traditional colour for reserve champion is purple. For horse classes, the ribbon or sash is placed around the horse's neck. For rider and turnout classes, the ribbon or sash is tied around your arm or across your shoulder. If you see a red/white/blue sash being tied around a horse's neck and the horse is being ridden, you are watching champion ridden class.

With experience, you will find it quite easy to keep track of which class is which. Until then, don't be embarrassed to ask other competitors – most people hanging around the entrance to the ring can tell you which class the ring is up to.

Rules

Most horse shows are run under the rules of the Equestrian Federation of Australia, but you may not need to be an EFA member to compete. A copy of the rules can be purchased from EFA or downloaded from their website. You don't need to be an EFA member to purchase the rules.

Royal shows and many large agricultural shows have their own rules under which the show will be run. These rules are available directly from the show societies, and will be similar to the EFA rules.

Shows or classes which are restricted to riding or pony club members will be run under the rules of the applicable association. These rules can be purchased from the pony/riding club association or downloaded from their website.

Hacking/showing summary

Hacking is popular and an excellent starting point for equestrian sport, especially for children and beginners. It can sometimes be frustrating, however, as judging is based primarily on an individual judge's opinion rather than on a set of specific criteria. You may have bad days, but overall you will be rewarded for your efforts and the best entrant will win most of the time.

Don't begin thinking that you are always getting beaten by Joe Bloggs because they have a new saddle/bridle/helmet and you don't. Rather, Joe Bloggs may simply ride better than you and their horse may perform better than your horse. Don't waste your money buying unnecessary equipment. Spend it instead on lessons with a good instructor, to improve your performance and your horse's performance. It's a much better investment.

3

Dressage

Dressage is an ancient sport that grew from the need to train horses to perform specific tasks on demand as part of battle. As horses' importance in warfare and day-to-day life diminished, the modern sport of dressage developed. The word 'dressage' comes from the French verb 'dresser' which means 'to train' and is defined as 'the art of training a horse in obedience, deportment and responses'.

Dressage is one of the three equestrian disciplines contested at the Olympic Games. Dressage classes are usually conducted at specific dressage competitions and sometimes at agricultural shows.

In the sport of dressage, a horse and rider perform a specific series of movements in an arena. The competition arena has a series of letters around the outside, about 1 m from the arena fence. A dressage test specifies which movements a rider must make at each letter (see Appendix 2 for an example). The horse and rider are judged on the accuracy and quality of their movements. What constitutes quality and accuracy in a dressage test is specified in the rules governing the sport. The beauty and presentation of the horse and the quality of the rider's clothing and equipment are *not* judged in a dressage test.

The judge gives a mark out of 10 for each movement, and may provide some remarks on why that mark was awarded. The marks are added and expressed as a percentage of the total marks available. The higher the percentage, the better the performance.

The sport of dressage is governed internationally by the International Equestrian Federation (FEI). In Australia, the Equestrian Federation of Australia (EFA), pony club association or riding club association controls the sport and provides rules and guidelines (based on the FEI rules) for official and associate competitions.

Levels of dressage competition

Competitors at dressage competitions compete according to their grading, not their age or their horse's height as is done in hacking/showing. In dressage, riders of different ages, riding horses of different heights, compete against each other. The grading levels depend on the organisation running the competition. Approximate grading equivalents are shown in Table 3.1.

Grand Prix is the highest level of dressage, Olympic level. The difficulty and quality of the movements that the horse has to perform get progressively harder from Grade 5 pony club, where the rider may only be required to walk and trot, up to Grand Prix.

Riding club association competitions

Riding club competitions are a fabulous entry-point into the world of dressage. Riding club associations have their own grading system and their own dressage tests. Riding club competitions are usually run by a riding club, under the rules of the state's riding club association. You must read the riding club association dressage rules before competing. The basics of a riding club competition are:

- the competition is approved as an official riding club competition by the riding club association
- the test is usually judged by a single judge, but at major competitions there may be two judges
- the judges may need to be accredited by the riding club association to judge at the specific level
- the arenas may be Olympic size (60 m × 20 m) or 40 m × 20 m, depending on the dressage level
- riders do not have to be registered with the EFA
- riders must be a member of an affiliated riding club
- horses will receive riding club grading points for performances at these competitions
- results in riding club official competitions are accepted as qualifications for riding club national and state championship competitions.

When a horse and rider join a riding club, a level assessor will grade them *as a combination*. A horse does not necessarily start in the lowest grade and work their way up. A horse may be graded above Grade 5 even if it has never competed, depending on the horse and rider's ability. If the horse is sold to another rider the

Table 3.1: Equivalent gradings for dressage

EFA (incl. FEI)	Riding club	Pony club
Grand Prix (FEI)		
Intermediate II (FEI)		
Intermediate I (FEI)		
Prix St Georges (FEI)		
Advanced		
Medium	Advanced	
Elementary	Level 1	
Novice	Level 2	Grade 1
Preliminary	Level 3	Grade 2
Preparatory	Level 4	Grade 3
	Level 5	Grade 4
		Grade 5

assessor will grade the new combination – at riding club level, unlike official dressage, the points gained by the horse with one rider do not remain with the horse for the new rider.

Once a horse and rider have been graded they gain points by achieving places at riding club competitions. As the combination earns more points they move up the various grades. A combination may compete at their level of grading or one grade higher, but they can't compete at a lower grade.

> **TIP:** A horse and rider combination will be given a separate grading for each discipline. These gradings need not be the same. A horse/rider combination that is particularly good at dressage and weaker at jumping will have a higher grading for dressage than showjumping.

Pony club association competitions

Pony club association competitions operate in much the same way as riding club association competitions, with one major exception – a pony club rider must attend a specific number of pony club rallies each year to be eligible to compete in official pony club competitions. Pony club riders are not permitted to compete at a higher or lower grade than their official grading.

Schools competitions

This type of event is relatively new to the equestrian landscape. Competitions are often run by schools which offer an equestrian program as part of their curriculum. The events generally use EFA dressage tests but are not official competitions. Neither horses nor riders are graded for schools competitions; competitors simply select their preferred level of competition. There is an honour system under which riders are expected to compete at their equivalent pony/riding club level. For example, a rider in Grade 1 for pony club would be expected to compete at novice level in schools competitions.

Associate EFA competitions

The size of associate EFA competitions can vary dramatically. Some are very small events with few competitors, while others are quite big. The size of the competition largely depends on where it is held – as a general rule, the further away from a capital or large regional city, the smaller the competition.

Associate EFA competitions use the same rules as official EFA competitions with a few fundamental differences:

- EFA has not classified it as an official competition
- only one judge is required
- the judge must be qualified to judge at the specific level
- the arenas may be Olympic size (60 m × 20 m) or 40 m × 20 m, depending on the dressage level
- the rider must be an associate member of EFA *or* a member of the club running the competition
- the horse does not have to be registered with EFA
- if the horse is registered with EFA, it cannot compete below its EFA level
- horses of any height and riders of any age are eligible to compete
- no points are earned towards the horse's grading
- performances don't count as qualification towards state or national championships.

Although there are no rules governing who can compete at an associate competition, it is an unwritten rule that if a horse or rider combination is competing successfully at official competitions they should not compete at an associate competition. Riders who compete officially often take a young horse to an associate competition, or ride at an associate competition when they are having their first ride at a higher level. This is acceptable, but a successful official horse/rider combination competing at an associate competition is bad sportsmanship and frowned upon.

Some organising committees set their own rules to give everyone a fair go, for example by having specific classes for riders under a certain age. Several clubs run Masters competitions, where classes are only open to riders over 40, 50, 60 or 70 years of age.

Official EFA/FEI competitions

The standard of official competitions can vary dramatically; from the Olympics, world and national dressage championships at one end of the scale to an official competition held in a country town. Official competitions have the following fundamental characteristics:

- EFA has classified it as an official competition
- each class is judged by one, two or three judges depending on the level
- all judges must be qualified to judge at the specific level
- the arenas must all be of Olympic size (60 m × 20 m)
- all riders, horse owners and horses must be registered with EFA
- horses may not compete below the level they are graded
- horses must be over 14.2hh
- riders must be 12 yrs or older
- results in official competitions are accepted as qualifications for national and state championship competitions.

Official competitions are the highest level of dressage competition. Horses commence official competition with zero points. A horse must place from first to sixth *and* achieve a score greater than or equal to 55% to gain points (greater than or equal to 60% for preliminary and novice level). As the horse gains more points it moves up through the grades. A horse may compete at a level higher than its grading but may not compete at a level lower than its grading. For example, a horse that is graded novice can compete at elementary level but may not compete at preliminary level (see Table 3.1).

In official EFA/FEI competitions the horse is graded at a particular level, not the horse and rider as a combination. Under certain circumstances a horse may be downgraded one grade – an application must be lodged with EFA. Downgrading may be granted, for example, when an inexperienced or junior rider purchases an experienced horse.

> **TIP:** When buying a horse ask the owner how many EFA points the horse has and therefore what its grading is. If the horse is graded many levels above your ability, there is not much point buying it if you want to compete in official competitions. You will not be allowed to compete the horse at a level lower than its grading at official competitions.

> **TIP:** When you do want to ride your horse at a level below its graded level at an official competition, you can do so *hors concours* (HC). HC means non-competitive – the judges will judge your test but your score will not be considered for a prize. Your score will also not count towards grading points. If you see a rider/horse with HC next to their name in a program/scoreboard, that score will not be considered in the placings.

Ready to compete at an official EFA competition. The horse is wearing a double bridle, which is only allowed at medium level and above.

Special EFA competitions

EFA has introduced a number of competitions to improve the development of young horses and young riders in the sport of dressage. These classes are:

- pony dressage
- junior dressage
- young rider dressage
- young horse dressage.

Pony dressage
- Horses must not exceed 14.2hh
- Riders may compete from the beginning of the year in which they turn 12 until the end of the year in which they turn 16
- The rules and tests for official EFA dressage are used
- The pony earns grading points towards its pony dressage grade
- Tests are judged as in official competition.

Junior dressage
- Horses must be over 14.2hh
- Riders may compete from the beginning of the year in which they turn 12 until the end of the year in which they turn 18

- The rules and tests for official EFA dressage are used
- A horse may not compete below its official EFA grading
- No points are earned in junior dressage towards the horse's official grading
- Tests are judged as in official competitions.

Young rider dressage
- Horses must be over 14.2hh
- Riders may compete from the beginning of the year in which they turn 16 until the end of the year in which they turn 21
- The rules and tests for official dressage are used
- A horse may not compete below its official EFA grading
- No points are earned in young rider dressage towards the horse's official grading
- Tests are judged as in official competition.

Young horse dressage
- Horses must be over 14.2hh
- Classes are run for 4-, 5- and 6-year-old horses, with the horse's birth date taken as 1 August
- The rules for official dressage are used, with some additional rules
- Tests approved by EFA for young horse competitions are used
- At some competitions, up to three horses ride the test together, i.e. three horses in the same arena follow each other through the movements
- Tests are *not* judged the same way as an official dressage competition. The horse is given a score out of 10 for a number of criteria such as walk, trot etc. The horse is judged on its quality, movement, conformation, behaviour and potential as a dressage horse, and in many ways it is very much like a ridden class at a show. As such, a horse who makes a mistake may still win the class if it has greater potential as a dressage horse.

Ground rules

Where to park
There is generally a designated parking area. Unlike at hacking/showing competitions, you can't park close to the arenas – only the judges' cars are allowed anywhere near the arena. It is not as important in dressage to be near the competition area. You will usually be riding two classes at specific times, so you don't have to keep as close an eye on the progress of your arena as you do at a show.

Find yourself a spot close to a tap, the toilet or the administration building, so you don't have to carry your horse's water bucket very far!

What to do when you get there

When you enter a dressage competition you are allocated a specific time at which to ride your test. If you are not riding until late in the day, you may not have to arrive at the ground before lunchtime.

When you arrive (and after getting your horse settled) you need to report in to the organisers at the administration building. The organisers will tick your name off a list and review your EFA/pony club/riding club grading card (no card required for associate classes). For official and associate classes, they will also want to see your EFA membership (unless you are a member of the organising club riding in an associate competition where no EFA membership is required). At pony and riding club events, the organisers will keep your card until the class has finished. They will write details of any placings in your card and sign it before returning it to you.

At pony and riding club competitions the organisers will inspect your helmet to make sure it meets the required safety standard. Take your helmet when you report in.

Some organisers may give you a number to tie on yourself or your horse when competing, but most shows now require you to have your own number. Saddleries offer numbers that you can attach with Velcro or pins to your saddle cloth; you can buy a full range of numbers to use at different events. The program will say whether you have to provide your own number. Most competitions allow you to use your own numbers (which often look neater than the ones they issue), but when you report in you must check whether you are allowed to use your own. If you are attaching numbers to the horse's bridle or saddle cloth you *must* have two numbers, one on each side of your horse.

If you are riding two or more dressage tests on the day you will have the same number for both tests. If you are riding more than one horse on the day you will be given a different number for each horse.

> **TIP:** In some states horses are allocated an EFA competition number when they are registered. The horse uses that number at all competitions.

There are often several dressage rings side-by-side at a dressage competition, and the program will say which ring you are riding in. It is not always easy to tell which ring is which – there isn't always a number marking each arena – so it is a good idea to ask the organisers about the rings when you report in. You should also ask where the gear check is located.

Riding the dressage test

The gear check

At least 20 minutes prior to riding the dressage test you must report for a gear check. The gear checker will check that the equipment you are using meets the rules under which the competition is being run, for example you must have the correct equipment according to pony club rules when competing at a pony club competition. At pony club competitions the gear checker also checks the safety of the equipment.

If your equipment is not correct you will be asked to change it and report for another gear check prior to doing your test. Once you have passed your gear check, your name will be ticked off a list. You should report for a gear check before each test, although the gear checker may not inspect you the second time. At some competitions (usually pony club and riding club) a sticker may be placed on the back of your saddle, boot or helmet to show you have passed the gear check.

TIP: At official and associate competitions, the gear check ensures you are meeting competition rules and that the horse's welfare is not being compromised. It is not the role of the gear checker at these events to adjust any of your equipment (even tighten your girth) unless it is affecting the horse's welfare. Even if the gear checker suggests that you tighten your horse's noseband, for example, you don't have to do it unless you agree.

Reporting to the judge
You need to keep an eye on the ring in which you will be competing to see when it is your turn. You will *not* necessarily go in number order, for example number 37 may ride after number 82. Check your draw to see which number is before you. It is a good idea to find the rider before you in the warm-up area, so you are alerted when they go in the ring.

When the rider before you has finished their test (saluted to the judge) you are allowed to ride around the *outside* of your arena. *Don't* approach the judge yet. The judge is usually in a car at the end of the arena, in the driver's seat. A 'penciller' will be in the passenger seat. The penciller writes down the scores as the judge marks each movement so the judge does not have to take their eyes off the horse and rider.

When the judge has finished writing their comments on the previous rider's test they will wind down their car window to indicate that you may approach the driver's window to report in. There is usually enough time to trot around the arena once or twice before the judge is ready for you.

TIP: If your horse is a little hot (worked up), don't try to make it stand near the judge's car while the judge is finishing off the previous test. Trot around the arena or behind the judge's car if there is room. A nervous horse usually gets worse if it has to stand still.

The judge will confirm your name and number (make sure you are next, according to their list). They will also tell you what signal will start your test: most

Dressage arenas are often set up side-by-side like here. Note the judges' cars parked by the edge of the arenas. Photo: Berni Saunders, www.cyberhorse.net.au/tve

of the time the signal will be the car horn, but some judges ring a bell and others toot the car horn and wave their arm.

After reporting to the judge you must ride down the outside of the arena to the entrance at the letter A (see Appendix 1). Do a circle in this area (usually at a trot) until the judge gives the signal. You must *not* enter the arena until the judge gives you the signal.

> **TIP:** On windy days or if there are several arenas close together it can be difficult to tell which horn belongs to your judge. It is useful to have a friend nearby to confirm that it was your judge's horn that you heard. If you think you heard the horn but aren't sure, raise your arm and wave to the judge. The judge will wave back or toot again to confirm that it was their signal. If you are worried about other noise or are hard of hearing, tell the judge when you report in and ask them to wave as well as tooting.

Riding the test

Once the signal has been given you have a certain time in which to enter the arena – in official and associate competitions you have 45 seconds. The time varies between associations, so check your rule book. No matter what type of dressage competition you are competing in, the time allowed to enter the arena is *plenty.*

Don't rush. If you are about to enter and your horse is naughty, do another circle before entering. Once you enter the arena there is no turning back.

You must ride the movements in the order and at the markers specified in the test you have learnt. The vast majority of dressage tests require you to halt and salute at the start and end of the test. To salute, take both reins into one hand, lay your free hand by your side near your thigh and bow your head. If you are carrying a whip, always salute with your free hand, not the one carrying the whip.

If something goes wrong and you lose your way, don't panic. All riders have lost their way in a dressage test sometime in their career. If you go the wrong way the judge will signal with their horn or bell, and get out of their car. Go up to the judge and find out where you went wrong. The judge will tell you your mistake and where to restart the test. You will lose marks for the error. How many you lose depends on the competition – the rules at the top of the test sheet specify how many points you lose for each error. If you make too many errors (four, in an official competition) you will be eliminated.

Scores and prizes

After you have completed your test, the judge's sheet will be taken to scorers. They add the marks and convert them into a percentage of the total possible marks. Your score will be shown on a scoreboard (usually on the building you reported into) as a mark (or two marks if there were two judges) and as a percentage. If there are two judges the marks from each judge will be added then divided by two; this will then be shown as a percentage.

The highest percentage wins. After all the scores have been posted the winners and place-getters will be marked on the scoreboard. You can then collect the test sheet that the judge marked you on. You should always collect your dressage test as it shows the individual marks you received for each movement as well as useful comments from the judge. These are usually put on a table – ask the organisers. You can't collect your score sheet until all the results have been posted on the scoreboard.

In general, prizes go to six places and there is usually a presentation ceremony. You may be required to wear your riding attire to the presentation, and at big competitions the winning horse may also have to be presented. If you have won a prize, ask the organisers what they expect in terms of presentation.

TIP: If you have travelled some distance to a competition you may not be able to stay until all scores have been posted, especially if you were one of the first to ride in a class of 30 horses. You can usually give the organisers an envelope in which to send your judge's sheet (and grading card, for pony/riding club). However, if you have won a prize it is good manners to wait until the presentations and receive your prize in person.

> **TIP:** Some competitions are run as 'championship' or 'jackpot' events. At these, not only are prizes given for each separate test but there is also a major prize for the competitor who performed best in the two tests at each level. Some events give trophies or horse rugs to the championship winner.

What to wear/equipment

Even though your presentation and equipment is not specifically judged in a dressage competition, it is still important to present a good overall picture. Being neat, clean and tidy are key to a good dressage competition. If you ride in on a dirty horse, with your hair not tied back correctly and wearing a crooked tie, it is very distracting for the judge and does not create a good impression. You should always present yourself and your horse as well as you can. This includes plaiting your horse's mane for all competitions.

By presenting yourself and your horse correctly you are showing the judge that you have put effort into the test you are about to ride.

Riding club associations
- Official uniform of your club. This varies, but all clubs require an approved safety helmet.

Pony club associations
- Official uniform of your club. This varies, but all clubs require an approved safety helmet
- Use of spurs depends on your level of competition. Check your rule book
- Use of a whip depends on your level of competition. Check your rule book.

Schools competitions
- White, off-white or fawn jodhpurs/breeches
- School shirt, tie and jumper
- Your school may provide saddle cloths in school colours
- An approved safety helmet must be worn.

Official EFA/FEI competitions
Details of the official attire are published in the applicable rule book and are always under review. The guidelines below are a rule of thumb.

Preliminary to medium level
- White, off-white, fawn or similar jodhpurs/breeches, although white is the most popular

- Riding jacket (hacking jacket)
- Shirt and tie *or* stock *or* rat-catcher collar (a button-up collarless shirt, possibly with simple decorative embroidery, worn without a tie or stock)
- Riders under 18 must wear an approved safety helmet
- Riders over 18 may wear a bowler hat, hunt cap or approved helmet (at medium level a top hat is allowed if the horse is wearing a double bridle). Recent changes to insurance have meant approved helmets must be worn by all riders at all levels at most competitions, depending on the organising committee's insurance. Check the program
- Gloves (very important, you must wear gloves)
- Short black/brown or long black/brown leather or synthetic riding boots, or full-grain black/brown leather leggings with matching boots
- Spurs may be worn at all levels but must be worn whenever the horse is competing in a double bridle. Check your rule book for the type and length of spur allowed
- Dressage or short whip may be used.

Advanced level
- Riding wear as described for preliminary to medium level above, or formal attire.

Formal attire
- White, off-white or beige jodhpurs/breeches
- Black or dark-blue tailcoat
- Shirt and stock or tie
- Top hat or safety helmet. Recent changes to insurance have meant Australian Standards approved helmets must be worn by all riders at all levels at most competitions, depending on the organising committee's insurance. Check the program
- Gloves
- Long black riding boots (top boots). The boots do not have to be leather; synthetic top boots are fine
- Spurs must be worn.

FEI level
- Formal attire as described above. Leather leggings are not permitted at FEI level
- Dressage whips may not be used at FEI level at championship events.

Associate EFA/FEI competitions
- Dress as for official EFA/FEI competitions

Rider dressed in formal attire. Photo: OZ Equestrian Photography

- Many organising committees allow riders to wear pony/riding club uniform in associate classes. Check with the committee.

> **TIP:** When the weather is very hot the organising committee may permit riders to compete without their riding jackets or club jumpers. Find out whether you are officially allowed to compete without your jacket/jumper – don't assume that it's okay just because it's a hot day. You can warm up without your jacket/jumper, as long as you wear it for your gear check and when you compete.

Equipment

In all dressage competitions you are required to use an English-style saddle, not a western or stock saddle. The saddle can be a:

- dressage saddle (most commonly used)
- jumping saddle
- all-purpose saddle
- hunting saddle.

It can be made of leather or a synthetic material.

The horse must wear a bridle of leather or a synthetic material. It is best to have the bridle the same colour as your saddle but it doesn't have to be. Some riders like to dress up their bridles by decorating the browband with coloured ribbon. This is especially attractive at pony/riding club competitions where you can match the ribbon to your club colours. It is acceptable at all dressage competitions. Some riders add other adornments on browbands and nosebands (see Chapter 7).

In all dressage competitions, the horse must have a bit as specified in the association rule book. At pony club and the lower levels of riding club and EFA competition you are required to ride with a snaffle-type bit. There are many acceptable snaffle-type bits, but some types (such as the Spanish snaffle) are not accepted. At higher level competitions the horse must have a double bridle, with two bits in its mouth. No dressage competitions allow the use of hackamores (a bit without a mouthpiece) or a Pelham bit (see Chapter 7).

It is generally accepted in EFA competitions, although it is not a rule, that riders use a white rectangular saddle cloth. You can use any colour saddle cloth you like, and use a shaped saddle cloth if you like. In pony/riding club competitions you may be required to wear your club saddle cloth if it forms part of your club uniform. If not, you can use any saddle cloth you like. Check with your club.

Your horse is not permitted to wear boots or bandages during the competition although they are acceptable in the warm-up area.

Where to warm up

Read the program carefully. Some events have designated warm-up areas and other areas which are out-of-bounds. If you see a big open polo field which looks like a terrific place to warm up but no one else is riding on it, ask the organisers if it's available.

You are *never* allowed to warm up in the arena you are going to compete in on the day of the competition. You may not be allowed to warm up in the arena even if you arrive the day before, unless the organisers give you specific permission to do so.

In general, all competition arenas – your arena and those used by other classes – are off limits on the day of the competition. There may be a space set up as a practice arena, but this is rare. Usually there is a designated warm-up area a little away from the competition arenas.

It is very important not to ride within 15–20 m of an arena when someone is competing. This is a rule under some associations, and good manners for all competitions. It is especially important that you keep well away from the competition arenas when your horse is playing up. It is not fair to disturb someone else's test by riding your upset horse too near them. The only time you may ride near another arena is when you are riding up between two arenas to report to a judge. This is quite common.

TIP: In dressage, you can't share a horse on the day of the competition. This is an important difference between hacking/showing and dressage. When hacking/showing, any rider can ride any horse on the day of the event. Several different riders may even use the same horse in different rider classes! This is not allowed in dressage and eventing: only the person competing on the horse is allowed to ride it on the day of the competition (except for specific derby and young horse classes). If another person rides the horse, the horse will be eliminated from the competition.

TIP: At pony club competitions in some states, no one is allowed to ride your horse at any equestrian competition (including shows) and neither is anyone other than yourself allowed to lunge the horse. Check your rule book. You may be eliminated if someone else lunges your horse.

Programs and entries

Entries for dressage competitions must be sent prior to the competition. Most associations (EFA, pony club, riding club) have a dressage competition handbook or calendar on their website. Buy a handbook or download it from the website, so that you can see all the association competitions for the year. Schools competitions and associate competitions are not always included in a handbook. They may be advertised in rural newspapers or through the local schools, pony/riding clubs and saddlery stores.

The book/calendar will detail what classes are being run at each competition, the cost of each class, by what date entries must be received and other relevant information. Entries usually close two to three weeks before a competition, but at bigger events entries may close four to six weeks before the competition.

You are usually sent a copy of your dressage times four to five days before the event. For some competitions your times are not sent out; if so, the method for providing times is on the entry form/handbook. These competitions will either:

- provide a phone number for you to ring on a particular day to be given your starting times
- direct you to a website where you can look up your times
- send an email to you.

Dressage tests

When you are entering a dressage competition the handbook or entry form will specify which tests are being used at the event. There are usually four to five tests available at each level of dressage, and the organisers choose which tests they are going to use. For example, at preliminary level EFA competitions there are five tests – 1A, 1B, 1C, 1D and 1E. At novice level there are five tests – 2A, 2B and 2C etc.

There are often two tests at each level at an event, allowing competitors to ride two separate tests. It is very important that you know which tests you are doing so that you learn them ahead of time. You will need a copy of the test you are going to ride. Each association sells a book detailing all the tests for that association. Most associations change their tests every few years, so make sure you have the most recent test book. Dressage tests may be available online – check the association website.

If you find the prospect of memorising the test a little daunting, in some competitions you may use a caller. A caller may be used at official EFA (except national championships), associate EFA and riding club competitions. Callers are *not* allowed at pony club competitions or at FEI level. A caller stands outside the arena while you are riding the test and reads each of the movements from the test sheet as you go. Calling a test correctly is quite skilful and takes a lot of practice. If you are going to use a caller, make sure it is someone with a loud voice who has called a test before. If you expect any handy bystander to call your test it will just end in tears.

It is always best to learn your test and practise it many times at home. Even if you are going to use a caller you must still know the test; the caller is just there to jolt your memory.

Arenas

Dressage arenas are always one of two sizes: 40 m × 20 m or 60 m × 20 m. The smaller arena is generally used for the lower levels of riding and pony club. For official and associate EFA competitions, the smaller arena may be used for preparatory and preliminary tests. For all others the large arena is used.

At the top of the test sheet you are following it specifies the arena size. In some cases the test sheet will say '40 m × 20 m or 60 m × 20 m' – the organisers have a choice of arenas. Check the handbook to see whether they specify which arena they are going to use. If they don't, do ring and find out. It is very important to know which size arena you are using, as it affects the way you ride the test. Diagrams of dressage arenas are shown in Appendix 1.

Rules

Each association runs their competitions under their rules. You must have a copy of their rule book and read it before you compete. Rules often change and although the rules across the various associations are fundamentally the same there may be small differences, such as whether you can use spurs and whether you have to wear gloves.

Dressage summary

Many riders consider dressage to be the ultimate in horse training. It takes years to learn the skills to ride a successful dressage test and a lifetime to perfect them. Dressage requires a great deal of practice and dedication. You cannot expect your horse to perform as you would like unless you have put in the hours.

To have any hope of reaching your potential in dressage you must have regular coaching from an experienced and dedicated instructor. Remember: with skill, dedication, the right horse and a bit of luck, the sky is the limit in this sport. Riding for your country at the Olympics can always be your dream.

4

Eventing/horse trials

Eventing is the triathlon of the equestrian world. It originated in the military and is often considered the ultimate test of horse and rider. Eventing consists of three phases:

- dressage
- cross-country (speed and endurance)
- showjumping.

Eventing is one of the three equestrian disciplines contested at the Olympic Games. Eventing, horse trials, one-day events (ODEs) and three-day events (3DEs) are different ways of describing this sport.

A horse and rider, as a combination, must complete each phase. The combination that accumulates the fewest number of penalty points over the three phases is the winner.

An eventing horse and rider must possess the training and riding discipline of the dressage phase; the boldness, speed and endurance required for the cross-country phase; and the obedience, carefulness and soundness to jump a showjumping course. The dressage and showjumping phases are held as individual equestrian events. The cross-country phase is run only as part of a horse trials event – there is no such thing as a cross-country jumping event.

Eventing can be a confusing discipline for beginners, but once you have a basic understanding of the terminology it can often be very enjoyable. Australasian riders have had enormous success in international eventing and Australian and New Zealand horses are highly sought after in this sport.

The sport of eventing is governed internationally by the International Equestrian Federation (FEI). In Australia, the Equestrian Federation of Australia (EFA), pony club association or riding club association controls the sport and provides rules and guidelines (based on FEI rules) for official and unofficial competitions.

Types of events

Undoubtedly one of the most confusing aspects of eventing is the way the events are described. It is important to note that the name of an event does *not* really mean how many days the event takes! An ODE can be run over one or two or even three days, while most 3DEs are run over four days.

Historically, ODEs consisted of dressage, a cross-country jumping course and a showjumping phase. A 3DE required riders to complete the requirements of the ODE *plus* a steeplechase course and two roads-and-tracks courses as part of the speed and endurance phase. Growing concerns regarding horse and rider safety, combined with the extra costs required to run the steeplechase and roads-and-tracks phases, mean that these phases are now optional in 3DEs.

In reality, most 3DEs are run without the steeplechase or roads-and-tracks – even the Olympic event is now run without them. A 3DE is now differentiated from an ODE by its longer cross-country course and the fact that it must be held over three or four days (with two days of dressage).

To overcome the confusion, most events are simply described as horse trials. The program confirms the type of class and the number of days over which the class will be run.

As a general rule, 3DEs are held only in EFA/FEI competitions, and even then they are usually only held for grades Novice and above. All pony/riding club competitions are run as ODEs.

> **TIP:** Check the program carefully to see how many days the competition runs. It is not unusual for some grades to run all three phases on the same day and other grades to run over two days at the same event.

Phases of eventing competition

Dressage

Eventing dressage is run in the same manner and under the same rules as stand-alone dressage competitions (see Chapter 3), but there are a few important differences.

- In eventing dressage, dressage tests may not be commanded (called) – you cannot have someone reading the movements out loud while you ride the test

- Some rules (including FEI and EFA competitions) do not allow a whip to be carried during the dressage phase, although it can be used in the warm-up area
- All dressage points for eventing are recorded as *penalty points* – the lower the score the better the performance. To determine penalty points, the total good marks you received are taken away from the total number of points possible (as if you got 10 for each movement). Depending on the organisation's rules (EFA, pony club etc.) the total dressage penalties may be multiplied by a coefficient such as 0.6 to determine the final dressage penalties. A coefficient is used to decrease the impact of the dressage in the overall competition

Example
  Total marks available on test = 400
  Total good marks achieved = 300
  Penalties = 100
  × coefficient 0.6 = 60 dressage penalties
- Dressage is always ridden as the first phase in eventing competition.

Cross-country/speed and endurance

A cross-country course is a series of fixed natural-looking obstacles, usually set on undulating terrain. The course length will vary depending on the level of competition, with the highest levels covering more than 5 km.

A horse and rider combination must go between the red and white flags which mark each obstacle, in the correct direction. Each obstacle is numbered and the obstacles must be ridden in the correct order. Obstacles may include:

- jumps
- ditches
- water (that the horse has to go through)
- drops (where the horse has to jump off a bank).

Unlike showjumping, cross-country jumps are not designed to fall down if the horse hits them. If a horse hits a cross-country jump and the jump actually falls down, the rider does not incur any penalties.

In eventing/horse trials, the cross-country phase has the greatest impact on results – a mistake in the cross-country phase incurs a far greater number of penalties than an error in the dressage or showjumping arenas.

Cross-country penalties

Two types of penalties can be incurred riding a cross-country course – jumping penalties and time penalties.

A jumping penalty is incurred when the horse refuses – it stops in front of the obstacle. This may sound straightforward but there are pages of information on

Into the water on cross-country, with the rider wearing a large cross-country watch to check their speed.
Photo: OZ Equestrian Photography

what constitutes a refusal. In general, when a horse refuses to jump a fence the rider turns the horse around and attempts to jump it again. This is a refusal and will be penalised. If a horse stops momentarily in front of a fence then jumps from a standstill, it is not always clear whether this counts as a refusal. Under EFA rules, if the horse is stationary in front of the jump and then jumps, it is a refusal. The judge who is watching that jump will determine whether there has been a refusal.

There are two times set for a cross-country course:

- optimum time
- time limit.

The optimum time is the time allowed to complete the course before time penalties start being incurred. The time limit is the maximum time allowed to complete the course; if a rider exceeds that they will be eliminated. The time limit is usually twice the optimum time.

TIP: Some eventing competitions have introduced a rule that applies penalties to riders who finish too far under the optimum time. It aims to slow down horse/rider combinations in the lower grades to improve safety. Check your rule book to find out whether this applies.

The penalties for errors on the cross-country course vary from association to association and are constantly under review. Some of the penalties for cross-country under EFA rules are:

- 20 penalties – 1st refusal at an obstacle
- 40 penalties – 2nd refusal at the same obstacle
- elimination – 3rd refusal at the same obstacle
- elimination – 4th refusal over the whole course
- 0.4 penalties – for each second over the optimum time
- 60 penalties – fall of rider at an obstacle
- elimination – 2nd fall of rider at an obstacle
- elimination – fall of horse at an obstacle
- elimination – jumping a jump in the incorrect order or in the wrong direction
- elimination – exceeding time limit.

Check your rule book for details of the penalties which apply to your level of competition.

Showjumping

Eventing showjumping is run in the same manner and under the same rules as a stand-alone showjumping competition (see Chapter 5). In eventing competitions, each horse/rider combination is required to complete one round of showjumping. The course is not jumped against the clock – there is no benefit in going fast because riders don't get any bonus points. They will, however, incur time penalties if they exceed the optimum time.

Some of the penalties for showjumping under EFA rules at the time of writing were:

- 4 penalties – knocking down a fence
- 4 penalties – 1st refusal at an obstacle
- elimination – 3rd refusal over the whole course
- 1 penalty – each second over the optimum time
- 8 penalties – 1st fall of rider
- elimination – 2nd fall of rider
- elimination – jumping a jump in the incorrect order or in the wrong direction
- elimination – exceeding time limit
- elimination – first fall of horse.

Table 4.1: Approximate grading equivalents

EFA (incl. FEI)	Riding club	Pony club
4 star		
3 star – Advanced		
2 star – Intermediate		
1 star – Novice	Advanced	
Pre-novice	Level 1	Grade 1
Preliminary (unofficial)	Level 2	Grade 2
Introductory (unofficial)	Level 3	Grade 3
	Level 4	Grade 4
	Level 5	Grade 5

Check your rule book for details of the penalties which apply to your level of competition.

Levels of eventing competition

Competitors at eventing competitions compete according to their grading. Riders of different ages riding horses of different heights compete against each other. The grading levels depend on the organisation running the competition. Table 4.1 shows approximate grading equivalents. Grades range from Grade 5 pony club up to 4 star level, which is the highest level. Dressage tests get more difficult, jumps get higher and the cross-country course gets longer as the grade level increases.

Riding club association competitions

Riding club eventing competitions are growing, and are excellent for less-experienced adult riders. The riding club associations have their own grading system and their own eventing levels. Riding club competitions are usually run by a riding club.

The competitions are run under the rules of the riding club association of that state. These general rules are similar to those of EFA competitions but there are some fundamental differences regarding equipment etc. Check the riding club association eventing rules before competing. The basics of a riding club competition are:

- the competition is approved as an official riding club competition by the riding club association
- the judges are accredited by the riding club association to judge at the specific level

- there is no need to be EFA registered
- the rider must be a member of an affiliated riding club
- horses receive riding club grading points for performances at these competitions
- results in riding club official competitions are accepted as qualifications for riding club national and state championship competitions.

When a horse/rider combination joins a riding club they are graded by an assessor at the club. A horse does not necessarily start in the lowest grade and work its way up. A horse may be graded above Grade 5 even if it has never competed, depending on the horse and rider's ability. If a horse is sold to another rider the assessor will grade the new combination.

Once a horse/rider combination has been graded they will gain points by achieving places at riding club competitions. As the combination earns more points they move up the various grades. A combination may compete at their level of grading or one grade higher. They may not compete at a lower grade.

> **TIP:** A horse/rider combination has separate gradings for dressage, showjumping and eventing. These gradings need not be the same – a horse/rider combination that is particularly good at dressage and weaker at jumping will have a higher grading for dressage than showjumping. A rider with a higher dressage grading than their eventing grading may be given a specific number of penalties in order to even out the competition. Details of penalties are in the riding club association rule book.

Pony club association competitions

Pony club association competitions operate in much the same way as riding club association competitions, with one major exception: a pony club rider must attend a specific number of pony club rallies each year to be eligible to compete in official pony club competitions. Pony club riders are not permitted to compete at a higher or lower grade than their official grading.

Training competitions

Training competitions can take many different forms. They may be run in conjunction with an EFA, pony club or riding club competition. Some examples of training classes are:

- training, maximum height 50 cm (as part of an EFA competition)
- training or Open Grade 2 (as part of a pony club competition).

Training competitions are generally open to all competitors, but organisers may restrict them to certain age groups. The committee specifies the rules under which the training competition will be run (EFA, pony club or riding club). It may also require riders to be an associate member of the EFA or the club running the event for insurance purposes. These requirements are usually set out in the program. If they aren't, make sure you ask.

The height of the jumps, length of the jumping courses and the dressage test are determined by the organising committee.

Training competitions are often held as part of pony club competitions and offer a wonderful introduction to eventing. Training competitions may be run down to Grade 5 for adult riders who are new to the sport but too old to compete at pony club level.

Unofficial EFA competitions (introductory/preliminary)

Unofficial EFA competitions use the same rules as official EFA competitions, with a few fundamental differences:

- the rider needs to be at least an associate member of the EFA
- the horse does not have to be registered with the EFA
- there are no qualification requirements to compete at introductory or preliminary levels.

Unofficial classes are the entry level into EFA eventing and are usually run as part of an official EFA competition.

Official EFA/FEI competitions (pre-novice and above)

Due to the time, money and effort required to run a horse trial event, there are far fewer events than showing, dressage or showjumping. Riders must meet the following age requirements to compete in senior official classes:

- 3 star and 4 star – beginning of calendar year in which they turn 18
- 2 star – beginning of calendar year in which they turn 16
- 1 star – beginning of calendar year in which they turn 14
- pre-novice – beginning of calendar year in which they turn 13.

At larger competitions there are specific official classes run for juniors and young riders:

- junior novice – 14–18 yrs (beginning to end of calendar year)
- junior pre-novice – 13–18 yrs (beginning to end of calendar year)
- young rider (any level) – 16–21 yrs (beginning to end of calendar year).

At a large competition there may be both a pre-novice class and a junior pre-novice class. They use the same dressage test and are run over the same jumping course, but prizes are awarded separately for senior and juniors/young riders. For example, a 15-year-old rider would have to decide whether to compete in the junior or open pre-novice class. It is the rider's choice, but there are usually few competitors in the junior class.

TIP: Rider age requirements are often under review. Check the rule book for current age requirements.

Official competitions have the following fundamental characteristics:

- EFA has classified it as an official competition
- all riders, horse owners and horses must be registered with EFA
- horses and riders must be qualified to compete at a particular level (not necessarily as a combination) (no qualification required to compete at pre-novice)
- horses may compete one level below that at which they are qualified, without penalty
- horses must meet minimum age requirements depending on the level of competition
- results in EFA/FEI official competitions are accepted as qualifications to compete at higher levels
- the maximum heights of jumps, length of jumping courses and dressage tests are set by EFA/FEI.

Official competitions are the highest level of eventing competition. Formerly, horses gained grading points by placing in official competitions. These points moved horses up the grades in a similar manner to that of official dressage competitions. In recent years this has changed to a system of qualification. Now, horses and riders (not necessarily as a combination) must meet certain criteria in a lower grade in order to compete in the next grade. The qualification regime is complex and is often refined by EFA and FEI. Check the current rule book for qualification requirements.

Ground rules

Where to park

There is usually a designated parking area. Make sure you park well away from any cross-country jumps – what seems like a nice spot in the morning might feel like a racetrack later as horses come galloping past on cross-country. It is good to park close to a tap, the toilet and/or the administration building to make it easier to carry water to your horse.

What to do when you get there

When you enter an eventing competition you are allocated a specific time at which to ride your dressage test. You are also told the time at which your class starts its cross-country and showjumping phases – you simply ride in numerical order from that start time.

After you get your horse settled, report in to the organisers at the administration building. They will tick your name off a list and view your:

- EFA/pony club/riding club grading card (no card required for associate classes)
- EFA membership card at official EFA competitions
- helmet
- medical armband
- back protector (in some cases).

Take all these items when you report in and save yourself a trip back to the car! The organisers will keep your riding/pony club card until the competition has finished.

The organisers will give you a number to tie on yourself or paper numbers to put into a back number-holder that you must provide. Check the program carefully or ask the organisers beforehand if you need to provide your own number-holder (all EFA/FEI competitions require you to have your own). Some organisers require you to use the large cross-country numbers for all phases of the competition, others let you use your own small numbers for the dressage and showjumping phases. Small numbers are allowed in dressage and showjumping at all official EFA/FEI competitions. Both the back number-holders and the small dressage/showjumping numbers can be purchased at most saddlery shops.

The organisers will give you a map of the cross-country course that you can use when walking the course.

There are often several dressage rings side-by-side – the program will specify which number ring you are riding in. However, it is not always easy to tell which arena is which, as they are not always marked with numbers. Check with the organisers which ring is which when you report in, and find out where the gear check and warm-up area are located.

Riding the dressage test

See Chapter 3 for details on riding the dressage test. The important differences between stand-alone dressage competitions and eventing competitions are:

- you are not allowed to have someone call the test at any horse trials event
- you are not allowed to carry a whip in EFA/FEI competition. Check the rule book for pony/riding clubs as rules vary from state to state
- you are not allowed to use rowel spurs for EFA/FEI competitions.

Don't forget your gear check 30 minutes before your test.

Multiple jumps are often set up side-by-side for each grade – make sure you know which is the correct one for your grade. The jump numbers for different grades are in different colours.

Riding the cross-country

Walking the course

A competitor is permitted to walk around the cross-country course to look at each jump and remember the course's direction. Under no circumstances is the horse to be shown any jumps or to practise jumping any prior to riding the course. Anyone who breaks this rule is eliminated. People who are not competing are also allowed to walk around the cross-country course, with a competitor or by themselves, and discuss the course with the competitor. You are allowed to walk the course more than once.

As several levels of competition are usually run at an event there are different coloured numbers on different jumps. Competitors are given a map to use when walking the course which will specify the colour for each level. Make sure you walk the correct jump for your coloured numbers. Don't be concerned if there are more than one coloured number on the same jump – it just means that riders from different grades jump the same jump.

There may be lots of numbers on a jump which seems higher than you were expecting. Don't panic. Check to see if there is a note attached to the jump which says the jump will be lowered for your grade.

There will be a red and white flag beside each obstacle. Competitors *must* go between these flags in the correct direction. *Red* is always on your *Right*. To work out the direction, find the correct coloured number for your grade. Your red flag is attached to the same part of the obstacle as the number.

Although walking the course at lower grades is fairly straightforward it is less simple as you move up the grades. To inexperienced riders, some combination obstacles with multiple options can look like a sea of red and white flags. It is essential to walk the course with someone who has cross-country experience to help you understand tricky jumps.

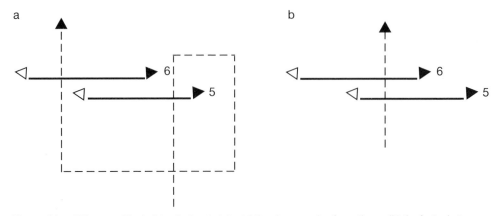

Figure 4.1: Riders need to decide whether to take (a) the slower and safer option or (b) the faster but riskier option. The slower option means less risk of jumping penalties but greater risk of time penalties. The faster option means greater risk of jumping penalties but less risk of time penalties.

> **TIP:** Make sure you count every jump. Sounds simple? Nearly all top riders have been eliminated for missing a jump sometime during their career.

At higher grades, some jumps are set out in such a way that you can take more than one route over the same jump. These routes are known as options. Option fences are usually designed to have a more difficult and fast option and a slower easier option (Fig. 4.1). The more direct route is usually in a straight line, while the slow route requires the horse to turn and to cover a greater distance, which affect the time taken. Riders must weigh up the risk of their horse possibly refusing the harder jump against the benefit of a faster time. At lower grades, time penalties rarely come into play so riders should choose the option they are most comfortable with.

> **TIP:** Make sure you know both options at the obstacle if you are intending to ride the fast option. If your horse refuses at the fast option, you can ride the slow option to avoid a second refusal.

The gear check

A gear check is not required for the cross-country phase of EFA/FEI competitions but it *is* required for all pony club and riding club competitions.

At least 20 minutes prior to riding the cross-country, you should report for a gear check. The gear checker will check that your equipment meets the rules under which the competition is being run, for example you must have the correct equipment according to pony club rules when competing at a pony club competition. At pony club competitions the gear checker will also ensure the safety of the equipment.

If your equipment is not correct you will be asked to change it and report for another gear check prior to doing your course. Once you have passed, your name will be ticked off a list. At some competitions (usually pony and riding club) a sticker may be placed on the back of your saddle or helmet to show you have passed the gear check.

Starting the course

At the end of the cross-country course your horse will be inspected by a vet to ensure its heart rate is acceptable and it hasn't sustained any injuries. Take a bucket, sponge, scraper and a drink for yourself to the vet check area *before* you begin riding, so it is ready when you finish the course. Eventing is one discipline where a helper (groom) is a great asset, especially at the end of the cross-country course when your horse needs a lot of attention.

At the start of the course there may be an enclosure called a start box. It is fully open on one side (the direction you start the cross-country) and may be partially open on the opposite side. Attached to the box is a red and a white flag, and a sign saying 'Start'. If there is no start box there will be a set of red and white flags with a sign saying 'Start'.

The starting judge sends horses out onto the course at regular intervals, usually one to three minutes at the lower levels of competition. You ride the course in numerical order, so keep an eye on the rider you are following.

The judge calls out something similar to 'Rider 23, you have 30 seconds'. At your 30-second warning you move to the start area. You do *not* have to stand in the start box – in fact once a horse has done one or two cross-country courses it is often impossible to get them to stand in the start box. Simply keep your horse moving near the starting area. If there is no start box, don't go through the red and white flags. If there is a box you *are* allowed to go between the red and white flags (in the wrong direction) to enter the box. As the box is closed on three sides this is the only way to enter it.

The judge calls you again 10 seconds before your start time, and counts down from 5 seconds to 'Go'. Your time starts from when the judge says 'Go', not from when you pass between the red and white flags.

How you manage your start largely depends on your horse. Some horses get so excited at the start of the cross-country course that their riders need to use all their skills just to get through the start flags. Most are fine once out on the course. Do whatever you need to keep your horse and yourself calm at the start. Some options are:

- enter the start box and face the horse to the back of the box until the judge says 'Go', and only then turn the horse around and through the flags
- if there is no back on the start box or no start box at all, walk towards the flags as the judge counts down from 5 seconds. You are *not* allowed to make a running start

In the start box ready to take on the cross-country course.

- have a helper hold the horse in the start box until the signal to go
- where there is a back on the box, circle in front of the box and move into the box as the judge counts down from 5.

Don't race your horse out of the start box – you are not on the starting grid of a Formula 1 Grand Prix! Keep your nerves and adrenaline in check and move out of the box at a trot or slow canter, then increase your speed to establish a good rhythm.

Riding the course

Take it easy! 'Slow and steady wins the race' definitely applies to cross-country riding. At the lower levels of competition the optimum time and associated penalties rarely apply unless you have a refusal, which will slow down your overall time. If you ride at a nice steady canter there won't be any problem staying within the optimum time.

At the higher levels you do need to move at a reasonable pace to make the optimum time, but this doesn't mean riding flat out. Horses that finish within the optimum time are often those that don't appear to be going fast at all, while the ones that seem to be going flat out often have time penalties. This happens because the fast horse is pulling to go faster, so the rider has to slow it right down to jump safely. A horse that canters along in a good rhythm can jump without changing its stride and often ends up with a better time.

Most associations' rules allow riders to wear stopwatches so that they keep an eye on how they are travelling against the optimum time. Check your rule book to see if they are allowed at your competition. Saddleries sell special stopwatches with a very large display that is easy to see when cantering. Most riders set their watch for the optimum time and have it count down.

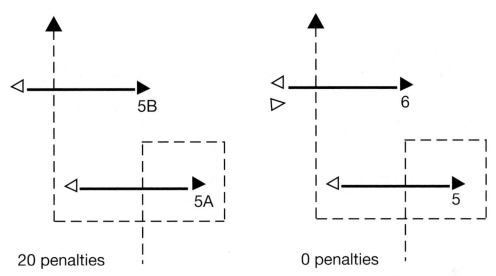

Figure 4.2: Take careful note of whether you are jumping a combination fence (5A, 5B) or two separate fences (5, 6). The numbers determine your options. When riding a combination fence, you cannot cross your track or you will incur penalties. You will not incur penalties if you cross your track between two fences that are not a combination.

Make sure you follow the course you walked and always count the number of jumps. It is very easy to accidentally miss a jump! If your horse has a refusal, take your time to turn around and try again. If your horse refuses the same jump three times or has five refusals across the whole course you are eliminated and must leave the course at a walk. You cannot continue jumping.

> **TIP:** If your horse refuses the second or third element of a combination fence, you do not have to jump the first element again. For example, if there is a combination marked 5A and 5B and your horse jumped 5A but refused 5B, you do not have to jump 5A again although you are allowed to do so if you want. In showjumping, if you have a refusal at part B you must re-jump part A.

At the lower levels riders sometimes catch up to each other on the course, particularly when a horse has had a refusal. If you catch up to another horse, call out for the rider to move aside and let you pass. This is especially important if they have stopped at a jump you are trying to jump. Common-sense rules apply to overtaking – overtake only when it is safe to do so, and don't force your way past another horse in a dangerous way. If another rider has caught up to you, you must give way – the rider behind you has right of way. Give the faster rider a clear distance – you can be eliminated for following another horse too closely around the course.

If there is an accident on the course ahead of you, or if you have been eliminated and are not aware of it, a judge may try to stop you by standing in your path and waving a flag. You *must* stop. If a judge has no flag and simply waves their

Cooling down horses in the vet check area after completing the cross-country course.

arms, you still stop. Make a note of the time that you were stopped, on your stopwatch, and the time they let you start again. The judge will also record this time but it is good to note it yourself in case they make an error. When your score is calculated the judges will take into account the time that you were forced to stop, so it's not included in your time.

> **TIP:** If you have outside assistance while riding the course you will be eliminated, regardless of whether or not you asked for the help. Common examples are:
>
> • calling or signalling directions to a rider on the course
> • having someone positioned at an obstacle to encourage the horse to jump.
>
> Cheering, clapping and general encouragement from spectators is fine. Catching a horse after a rider has fallen off, helping the rider remount and handing a whip or spectacles to a rider are allowed and will not cause elimination. Check your rule book for details of 'outside assistance'.

Finishing the course

The end of the course is marked by a red and white flag and a sign saying 'Finish'. You must ride between the flags in the correct direction to finish the course. Once you have passed through the flags, immediately move away from the finish line to the vet check area. You will be eliminated if your horse's welfare has been affected, for example if its heart rate is too high after a set rest period or if it is injured or lame.

In the vet check area there is a marshal who organises the riders. They are usually the person with the clipboard. In pony club competitions you can't dismount without permission from the marshal. If they don't tell you to dismount, ask if you can do so.

Once you are off your horse, loosen its noseband and girth. Take the saddle off if you like, but if so you'll have to carry it back to the float yourself. Sponge your horse and make it comfortable, especially if it is a hot day. Don't be concerned if your horse won't have a drink. Most horses are too excited at the end of the cross-country to drink straight away, but will have one back at the float or yard. Walk your horse around the vet check area until your number is called. The vet will listen to your horse's heart and may ask you to lead the horse at a trot to make sure it isn't lame. If the horse has a high heart rate you might be asked to wait another five minutes or so, after which the vet will then check it again.

When the vet is satisfied with your horse's health they will tell you to leave. If they aren't satisfied they will explain why and may eliminate you from the competition.

Riding the showjumping

See Chapter 5 for details on riding the showjumping course. A gear check may be required for this phase – check your program or ask the organisers. In eventing, some organising committees allow you to complete the showjumping phase even if you were eliminated in the cross-country phase. It is good practice to do the showjumping even if you are out of the competition.

Scores and prizes

As each phase of the competition is completed your scores will be posted on a scoreboard, usually on the building you reported into. The scores for each phase are written in separate columns. Usually, jumping and time penalties are shown separately for both the cross-country and showjumping phases.

The lowest score wins, i.e. the competitor with the fewest penalties. After all scores have been posted, the winners and placegetters will be marked on the scoreboard along with a note saying what time the final scores were posted.

If you want to dispute the results, you can do so within 30 minutes (the time depends on the rules of the association). The dispute may involve a scoring error by the committee, for example they accidentally applied a penalty to you instead of another rider, or be related to a judge's decision on the cross-country or showjumping course.

As discussed earlier, it is not always easy to judge whether a competitor jumped an obstacle without incurring a penalty. You may think you did but the judge may say that, for example, your horse took a backward step before taking the jump. To dispute a score, you must get all your facts together and approach the organisers within the designated time frame.

In general, prizes go to 6th place and there is a presentation ceremony. If you have won a prize you may be required to wear riding attire (including helmet) to the presentation. At big competitions, the winning horse may also have to be presented. Check the program or ask the organisers what they expect of prizewinners with respect to the ceremony.

What to wear

Dressage

Details of what to wear are given in Chapter 3. In eventing dressage, just like stand-alone dressage, even though your appearance is not specifically judged it is good manners to present yourself and your horse well. Dress requirements are the same as for stand-alone dressage except for the higher levels of EFA/FEI competition. Check your rule book to determine at which EFA/FEI eventing levels you can wear formal attire.

Cross-country

- An approved safety helmet is compulsory for cross-country riders – the required standard is set by the association running the competition. Check that your helmet is the correct standard according to the current rules and fits correctly. Standards change, and a helmet that was acceptable last year may no longer be acceptable
- Anyone with long hair must tie it up when riding cross-country. Hair that hangs over your back number makes it very difficult for the jump judge to see the number. Even a long plait can obscure your number. If you have long hair, roll it up right out of the way
- Safety vests (back protectors) are allowed at all levels, and are compulsory for EFA competitions. Safety vests provide additional back protection in case of a fall and most riders now wear them for cross-country
- Riders must wear jodhpurs/breeches and long boots. Juniors can wear short boots. Boots can be leather, rubber or leather leggings
- Riders are encouraged to wear comfortable lightweight clothing known as cross-country 'colours'. Commentators and spectators can recognise riders at a distance by their colours. Experienced competitors generally wear lightweight jockey silks and matching hat covers. Many have worn the same colours for years and are very easy to recognise. For beginners, a rugby top or polo shirt is fine. All colours are acceptable except for green and gold, which can only be worn by Australian representatives while riding for Australia
- Riding club and pony club competitors are generally required to wear their uniform but some competitions allow you to wear cross-country colours or polo shirts. Ask your club or check your rule book

A pony club rider on cross-country. The rider's back protector can be seen under her cross-country number.
Photo: Julie Wilson Photography

- Spurs are allowed at all levels of EFA/FEI competition and most higher pony club and riding club levels. Check your rule book for any exceptions
- Competitors may carry a short whip, but long whips (dressage whips) are not allowed. Check your rule book for the maximum length
- All riders must wear a large back number that can be seen by jump judges. For all EFA and some other competitions you must provide your own back number-holder, and the organisers provide a paper number to slide into the holder. For other competitions you will be given a back number similar to a netball bib. The program will say whether you must provide your own back number-holder. If in doubt, ask before the event
- All riders must wear a medical armband while competing. These can be purchased from your association and some saddleries. The armband contains details of emergency contacts and any pre-existing medical conditions.

TIP: Always remove the paper number from your number-holder after the competition. If you leave the number inside, the ink will transfer to your transparent holder and leave a permanent mark on the plastic.

> **TIP:** If you are buying a set of jockey silks for cross-country avoid choosing a colour or design already worn by a prominent rider. Your back number and back protector will cover a large part of your silks, so choose a design with interesting hat cover and sleeves that will remain visible when you are riding.

Showjumping
- EFA – as per eventing dressage with safety helmet. Formal attire is never worn in the showjumping phase
- Riding club – club uniform
- Pony club – club uniform.

Equipment
Always check your rule book for specific saddlery requirements. The information here is only a general guide.

Dressage
- See the details given in Chapter 3. Saddlery requirements are the same as for stand-alone dressage.

Cross-country
- The type of saddle you use during cross-country is optional, but a jumping saddle is best
- Many riders match their saddle cloth colour to their cross-country colours but this is purely for aesthetic purposes. Any saddle cloth is acceptable. Pony club/riding club members may be required to use their club saddle cloth if it is part of their official uniform
- You must use a bridle (leather or synthetic) and there must be reins attached to the bit or bridle
- All bits are allowed, except for hackamore bits in pony club competition
- Running martingales, Irish martingales and breastplates are allowed. You can't use a standing martingale, running reins or anything else that restricts the horse
- An overgirth is recommended, as a safety girth in case your regular girth breaks. An overgirth is compulsory if your saddle only has a single girth strap
- Boots for your horse are allowed in cross-country and it is a good idea to use them. Boots protect a horse's legs if it hits a jump. Choose a boot which is closed both in front and back to protect your horse's leg all the way around. Your saddlery shop can help you choose the correct type of boot.

TIP: When purchasing cross-country boots for your horse always bear in mind what they are going to be put through. A leather boot with woollen lining looks great in the shop but won't look nearly as nice after it has been through the mud and the water jump. You want a tough boot that won't tear easily or absorb too much water, while still providing good protection.

- Studs are acceptable during all phases of a horse trials competition. They give a horse additional traction in slippery conditions. Studs are similar to football boot stoppers that screw into the horse's shoe. A farrier will have to make the necessary holes in your horse's shoes – ask your farrier in advance so they can bring the necessary equipment. Most riders put two studs in each back shoe and one stud on the outside of each front shoe. When and which studs to use is a personal choice – experienced riders often carry boxes of different size studs for different conditions. If you are unsure, ask your instructor or a more experienced rider on the day what they are using. If in doubt, don't use any!

TIP: Putting studs into a horse's shoes is a rotten job and always takes longer than you think. Put them in as early as possible, but obviously not before you put the horse in the float or you will get unwanted drain holes in the floor. Definitely put them in before you get into your riding clothes! Stud kits include a small tool to clean the dirt out of the stud holes. It is very easy to accidentally cross-thread the holes with this tool, so do it carefully. If you cross-thread a hole, it becomes useless. You can buy little plugs which screw or push into empty holes, which are well worth using as they keep the holes clean and make your job a lot easier.

Showjumping
- See the details given in Chapter 5. Saddlery requirements are the same as for stand-alone showjumping *except* that standing martingales are not allowed in the showjumping phase of a horse trials event.

Where to warm up
You are *never* allowed to warm up in the arena you are going to compete in on the day of the competition. You may not be allowed to warm up in the arena even the day before, unless the organisers give specific permission to do so. This applies to both showjumping and dressage arenas.

There is usually a designated warm-up area for the dressage phase near the competition arenas. Don't warm up for dressage too close to any of the cross-country jumps – you may be eliminated for showing your horse the jump before the cross-country phase. See Chapter 3 for further details on where to warm up for dressage.

For cross-country and showjumping there will be a practice jump set up near the showjumping arena and at the start of the cross-country course. You are allowed to jump these as often as you like, but most horses perform best with just a couple of goes over the practice jump. The practice jumps will have a red and white flag. Make sure you jump in the correct direction, keeping the red flag on your right, to reduce the risk of collision.

Programs and entries

Entries for eventing competitions must be made prior to the competition. Each association (EFA, pony club, riding club) has a horse trials handbook and/or an event calendar on its website – buy the handbook or download the calendar. They will show all that association's competitions for the year. They specify what classes are being run at each competition, the cost of each class, the date by which entries must be received and other relevant information. Entries for most competitions close two to three weeks before the competition, but for bigger events entries may close four to six weeks beforehand.

You are usually sent details of your dressage time and the start time for your level's cross-country and showjumping phases four to five days before the event. Some competitions don't send out times. If so, the method for providing times is shown in the entry form/handbook:

- a phone number to ring on a particular day to be given your starting times
- a website where you can look up your times
- an email sent to you.

Dressage tests

The handbook or entry form will specify which tests are being used at a horse trials competition. There are several tests at each level of dressage, and the organisers can choose which ones they are going to use. For example, at pre-novice level EFA horse trials the committee can choose a dressage test from the four available at novice level (novice-level tests for stand-alone dressage are used at pre-novice level horse trials).

It is vital to know which test you will face so that you can learn it ahead of time – you can't have someone call a horse trials dressage test. Each association sells books with all the tests for their association, for example there is a book of tests for pony club competitions and a separate book for riding club competitions. Most associations change tests every few years, so make sure you have the most recent test book. You may be able to download the current tests from a website.

Arenas

See Chapters 3 and 5 for information regarding arenas. The standard of eventing dressage arenas varies dramatically from venue to venue, from beautiful sand arenas to cowpat-covered paddocks sloping downhill. You need to be ready for anything!

Rules

Each association runs their competitions under their rules. It is essential to read the rule book before you compete. Rules often change and although the basic rules are fundamentally the same, there are always small differences, such as whether you can use spurs and whether you have to wear gloves.

Eventing summary

Eventing is the equestrian sport that gets your blood and adrenaline pumping. It is an exciting and exhilarating sport but it can also be dangerous. Never underestimate the risks associated with cross-country riding and make sure you and your horse are well prepared for the task.

Speed is often the biggest danger to a horse and rider on cross-country. If your horse gets too fast or out of control on the cross-country course, you shouldn't be attempting a horse trials event. Parents and beginners are often misled into buying dangerous horses that go flat-out on the cross-country course by being told that the horse 'loves to jump'. A horse that loves to jump is often the most dangerous horse. It will stop at nothing – a horse that jumps no matter what can be disastrous. You are far better off with a horse that will refuse a fence if you present it incorrectly.

With the right horse and the right instructor you may follow in the footsteps of some of Australasia's best riders, who have made it to the top of the eventing world.

5

Showjumping

The first showjumping competitions were 'leaping' competitions where a horse and rider attempted to clear a single jump. Similar to human highjumping competitions, the horse and rider who could jump the highest (or widest) jump was declared the winner. A highjump type of class (the puissance) still exists in modern showjumping, but it is rarely held. The vast majority of showjumping competitions consist of a series of obstacles set out in a specific formation.

Showjumping is one of the three equestrian disciplines contested at the Olympic Games. Showjumping competitions may be run as part of a horse show or as a stand-alone showjumping competition.

A horse's natural ability to jump high is only one factor in successful showjumping. It is equally important to school the horse to obey commands to adjust its speed and length of stride.

Show jumps consist of light timber rails which sit in small brackets called cups, attached to stands called 'wings'. The rails are designed to fall from their cups if the horse touches them, in much the same way as a highjump or polevaulting rail will fall.

The sport of showjumping is governed internationally by the International Equestrian Federation (FEI). In Australia the Equestrian Federation of Australia (EFA), pony club association or riding club association controls the sport and provides rules and guidelines (based on FEI rules) for official and unofficial competitions.

Levels of showjumping competition

At a showjumping competition horses and riders compete according to their grading. Riders of different ages riding horses of different heights may compete

Table 5.1: Approximate grading equivalents

EFA (incl. FEI)	Riding club	Pony club	Approx. maximum height of jumps
World cup			160 cm
A Grade			150 cm
B Grade		A Grade	140 cm
C Grade	Advanced	B Grade	120 cm
D Grade			110 cm
	Level 1	C Grade	105 cm
	Level 2	D Grade	90 cm
	Level 3	E Grade	75 cm
	Level 4		60 cm
	Level 5		45 cm

against each other. The grading levels depend on the organisation running the competition. Table 5.1 shows approximate grading equivalents. Check your rule book for detailed specifications of each grade.

'A' grade or world cup is the highest level of showjumping competition, Olympic level. Not only the height of the jumps increases as you move up through the grades; the width of the jumps, the technicality of the course and the speed at which you must complete it also increase.

Freshman/training events

Freshman/training events are often run in conjunction with a showjumping competition in a separate ring at the event, or as a stand-alone event. They give horses and riders practice at riding under competition conditions.

Freshman events are non-competitive – there is no winner. Each horse/rider combination simply has a turn at riding the showjumping course. Most events allow you to jump the course more than once if time permits. At some events, each combination that completes a clear round receives a ribbon.

A freshman event is an excellent place to start your showjumping career.

Riding club association competitions

Riding club showjumping competitions are growing and provide less-experienced adult riders and horses with great competition. Riding club associations have their own grading system and their own showjumping levels. Riding club competitions are usually run by a riding club and may be run as part of a riding club show or a combined training day. In a combined training competition, a horse/rider combination rides a dressage test and showjumping round and can incur penalty points as at a horse trials event. The combination with the fewest penalties is the winner.

Riding club competitions are run under the rules of the riding club association of that state. These rules are similar to those of EFA competitions but have fundamental differences with respect to course design, saddlery etc. Check the riding club association showjumping rules before competing. The basics of a riding club competition are:

- the competition will be approved as an official riding club competition by the riding club association
- there is no need to be EFA registered
- the rider must be a member of an affiliated riding club
- horses will receive riding club grading points for performances at official competitions
- results in riding club official competitions are accepted as qualifications for riding club national and state championship competitions.

When a horse and rider, as a combination, join a riding club, an assessor grades them. As in all riding club disciplines, the horse does not necessarily start in the lowest grade and work its way up. A horse may be graded above Grade 5 even if it has never competed, depending on the horse and rider's ability. If the horse is sold to another rider an assessor will grade the new combination – unlike EFA showjumping, the points gained by the horse with one rider do not transfer with the horse to the new rider.

Once a horse and rider have been graded they gain points by achieving places at riding club competitions. As the combination earns more points they move up the various grades. A combination may compete at their level of grading or one grade higher. They may not compete at a lower grade.

Pony club association competitions

Pony club association showjumping competitions operate in much the same way as riding club association competitions, except that a pony club rider must attend a specific number of pony club rallies each year to be eligible to compete in official pony club competitions. Pony club riders are not permitted to compete at a higher or lower grade than their official grading.

Unofficial EFA competitions

Unofficial EFA competitions use the same rules as official EFA competitions, with a few key differences:

- the rider needs to be at least an associate member of EFA
- the horse does not have to be registered with EFA
- no grading points are awarded

A pony club rider showing an excellent position over a show jump. Photo: Paws 4 a Moment

- the horse may be allowed to compete below its graded level (at the discretion of the organising committee, so check the program).

Unofficial competitions are the entry level into EFA showjumping.

EFA-affiliated competitions

Although the rules for EFA competitions are the same regardless of the event, the standard of the competition varies dramatically. Under EFA rules a horse starts its competition career without any grading points regardless of who is riding it – it doesn't matter whether the horse is being ridden by an Olympic competitor or a beginner. As the horse competes successfully at EFA-affiliated competitions it gains points and moves up through the grades. The points awarded are:

- 1st place – 4 points
- 2nd place – 2 points
- 3rd place – 1 point.

Table 5.2: EFA points needed to reach each grading level

EFA	Points
A Grade	80+
B Grade	40 to <80
C Grade	16 to <40
D Grade	<16

Points are only awarded at EFA competitions where:

- the competition had a jump height of at least 105 cm
- the horse was not in a junior or young rider class
- the prize money/goods was >$99
- there were at least 10 competitors
- the event wasn't a team event such as a relay.

TIP: When buying a horse, ask the owner how many EFA points the horse has and therefore what its grading is. If the horse is graded many levels above your ability there is not much point buying it if you wish to compete at official competitions. You aren't allowed to compete a horse at a level lower than its grading at official competitions.

TIP: Rider age restrictions are often under review and vary depending on the type of competition. Check your rule book for current age requirements.

Official competitions have the following fundamental characteristics:

- EFA has classified it as an official competition
- all riders, horse owners and horses must be registered with EFA
- horses may not compete below their grade but can ride at a lower level HC (non-competitive)
- horses (not riders) gain grading points
- horses must meet minimum age requirements depending on the level of competition
- results in EFA/FEI official competitions are accepted as qualifications to compete at higher levels
- the maximum heights/width of jumps, length of the jumping course etc. are set by EFA/FEI.

Official competitions are the highest level of showjumping competition. As with dressage, the standard of an EFA competition can vary dramatically. As a

View across a showjumping arena. Photo: Julie Wilson Photography

general rule, the most competitive showjumping competitions are at World Cup shows, royal shows and national and state championship events. Agricultural shows and local horse shows/gymkhanas (see definitions in Chapter 2) generally have a lower level of competition, with fewer competitors and jumps likely to be lower than the maximum height. Unlike other equestrian disciplines, the standard of a showjumping competition can generally be judged by the amount of prize money – the more prize money, the higher the standard of competition.

There is rarely a restriction on the number of competitors in a showjumping class, except for championship events requiring qualifications. It is not unusual to see 100 competitors in a single class at the lower levels at a big event. This can mean a lot of waiting around if you only have one horse to compete.

Types of classes

The different types of showjumping events are numerous, and associations often introduce new ones. The list below shows only some of the showjumping classes on offer.

Table A
- One jumping round only
- One timed round
- Fastest clear round wins
- If tied for first, then prize is split.

Table A.1

- Optimum time but not against the clock
- If more than one rider completes the course without penalty (clear round) they will do a second jumping round over a modified course (jump-off)
- There may be one or two jump-offs to determine the winner but not against the clock.

Table A.2

- Same as Table A except if equal first there is a jump-off to determine the winner.

Table AM.3

- Optimum time but not against the clock
- Equal first go into jump-off against the clock.

Table AM.4

- First round not against the clock
- Those with equal penalties into first jump-off, not against the clock
- If still equal, second jump-off but this time against the clock.

Table AM.5

- Time taken in the first round determines the minor placings
- If equal first, then a jump-off against the clock.

Table AM.6

- Same as AM.5 but if still equal after jump-off there is a second jump-off against the clock.

Table AM.7

- First round, optimum time but not against the clock
- If rider has clear round they must stay in arena and immediately complete jump-off once the bell is rung a second time
- Only one jump-off.

Table C

- Competitor is penalised in seconds for each penalty during the course, added to the number of seconds taken to complete the course
- No penalties for disobedience as the additional time taken to rejump the obstacle is the penalty
- 3 refusals = elimination
- May include a jump-off at the discretion of the organisers.

Jumping equitation

- Judged on the horse/rider's technique over the course
- Increasing in popularity, especially for younger riders to reward good technique and discourage riding too fast.

Fault and out competition

- Round finishes when first fault is incurred (refusal, knockdown etc) – if you knock down the first fence that is where you finish
- Points for correctly jumped obstacle
- Highest points wins
  - Set number of obstacles: set numbered course, if no fault then time taken to jump course decides winner; jump-off if equal
  - Fixed time: jump the course then rejump until time limit is reached or fault is incurred.

Hit-and-hurry

- 2 points for obstacle correctly jumped, 1 point for obstacle knocked down
- Competitors must jump as many jumps as possible in the set time; competitor with the highest points wins.

Top score

- Obstacles built so they can be jumped in both directions
- Each obstacle given 10–120 points depending on difficulty
- Competitors jump as many obstacles as possible (maximum twice over each jump) within time limit
- No points for a jump that is knocked down
- Bell is rung at end of the time. Rider must pass between finish flags as quickly as possible and time is recorded
- Joker fence may be jumped twice with double points but points are deducted if it is knocked down
- No combination jumps
- Time in case of equal points
- No penalties for refusals.

Take your own line

- Can start and finish in either direction
- All jumps must be jumped
- Run under a Table C.

Competition over two rounds

- Two rounds of competition over the same or different courses

- Winner determined by adding penalties from both rounds
- Jump-off against the clock to separate winners.

Derby

- Special competition run over a longer distance
- Must include minimum 50% natural obstacles
- Course is often over undulating ground
- Only one round with a shortened jump-off, stated in program
- Can be run under Table A or C.

Accumulator competition

- Run over six, eight or 10 obstacles
- Each obstacle is progressively more difficult
- Bonus points are awarded for each fence as follows: fence 1 = 1 point, fence 2 = 2 points etc.
- No bonus points for fence knocked down
- Faults other than knock-down penalised as per Table A
- Combinations with the fewest number of faults and the most bonus points is the winner.

Double accumulator competition

- Similar to accumulator
- Combinations with no faults in first round move into second round
- In the second round, points are deducted in the reverse order to which they were accumulated (higher points scored come off first) as each fence is knocked down
- Combination with the greatest number of points and the fewest number of faults over the two rounds is the winner
- Time in the second round determines the winner in the case of a tie.

Competition in two phases

- Two phases (courses) run consecutively, with the finishing line of the first competition being the starting line of the second competition
- Program with specific conditions under which the competition will be run
- Competitors who receive penalties or exceed the optimum time in the first phase don't move on to the second phase.

Optimum time competitions

- Run under Table A with one or two phases
- Time penalties added to jumping penalties for each second under or over the optimum time.

Ground rules

Where to park

If possible, park close to the ring in which you will be competing. Rings are often marked with a sign or flag. There is often a lot of waiting at a showjumping competition, especially if you are competing only one horse. Try to get a spot with a good view of the action but not too close to the entrance to the ring or to the practice jumps, where there is a lot of horse traffic.

What to do when you get there

Depending on the type of competition, you may have pre-entered the classes you intend to ride in. If so, for EFA events you are usually not required to report in. At pony club and riding club competitions you will need to report to the secretary and present your card, helmet and medical armband for inspection. If you haven't pre-entered you will need to see the secretary and advise which classes you wish to ride in.

At big competitions an official draw determines the order you ride in, but at many other competitions it is a case of first-in first-served. The secretary may have a list of horses and add to that list as entries are received. At some competitions there may be a blackboard where you write your horse's name. The steward of the ring will call out each horse's name from the blackboard, in turn, to ride the course.

It is important to arrive well before the start of the class you intend to compete in. Once the class starts you will not be allowed to enter the ring on foot to walk the course. Make sure you are there in plenty of time to walk the course (see below), even if you are not going to be riding until later.

> **TIP:** When a blackboard system is used to determine the order of riding, the board usually has start order numbers on one side and a line for your name on the other. You can put your name on any blank line – you don't have to put it on the next available line. When riders have more than one horse they may put one on line 5 and another on line 25, for example, to give themselves time between courses. If you write your name at number 15, this doesn't mean that you will necessarily be 15th to go unless there are the same number of riders as there are places. If no one writes their name above yours, you will be first to go even if your name is on line 15. Keep an eye on the board to work out where in the class you will be riding.

Riding the showjumping course

Walking the course

The rider is permitted to walk around the showjumping course on foot to look at each jump, to pace out the distance between the jumps and to remember the direction of the course. Under no circumstances is the horse allowed in the arena before the class. Neither can it be shown any of the jumps or jump any of them prior to riding the course. People who aren't competing are *not* allowed to walk around the showjumping course, but this is not strictly enforced at the lower levels of riding/pony club.

The course builder will advise when the course is ready to be walked. There may be a bell or an announcement by the course builder or the judge. If you are unsure whether the course is open for walking, ask the judge.

Riders are allowed to walk around the course as many times as they like while it is open. You will be told when the course is closing, and be asked to leave the arena if you are still finding your way around the course.

It is good manners, and a rule in some cases, that you wear correct competition riding attire while walking the course. If riding attire is not compulsory, your clothes must be at least neat and tidy. If you wear your riding attire you can't go wrong.

TIP: You will not be allowed to walk the course a second time (after the competition starts) if there is a jump-off, so walk the jump-off course as well as the main one before riding begins.

Each jump has a number, and sometimes a letter, attached to it. There is also a red and white flag that indicates the direction in which you must jump the fence (top score competition fences don't have red and white flags as you are permitted to jump the fence from either direction). There will be a set of red and white flags denoting the start and finish, which will be marked accordingly.

TIP: Make sure you count every jump in the right direction when you walk the course. Remember, the Red flag goes on your Right.

The gear check
A gear check is not required for EFA/FEI competitions but is generally required for pony club and riding club competitions. Check your rule book.

Starting the course
You may enter the arena when the rider before you has passed through the finish flags and the steward has opened the 'gate'. Not all arenas have a proper gate which is opened and closed for each rider – a 'gate' usually consists of a piece of rope hooked onto a star post. As there are often many competitors in showjumping competitions officials try to keep things moving by getting the next competitor into the arena as quickly as possible. It is normal to enter the arena while the previous competitor is leaving or jumping the last jump, if the gate is on the opposite side.

Walking the showjumping course. Photo: Major Tom Mouat MBE

Present yourself to the judge upon entering the arena. Ride to where the judges are sitting – at bigger competitions they may be in a judges' box but often they just sit in the back of a float on the edge of the arena. Salute the judges when you are in front of them. *Do not* remove your helmet (although riders used to in the past) – simply raise your hand to the peak of your helmet and bow your head. The judge will confirm your horse's name and acknowledge your salute.

When you are in the arena you may ride around the jumps but you must *not* deliberately show any jumps to your horse. If you try to give your horse a look at a fence you may be eliminated. You may continue to ride around the course at any pace until the judge signals you to start by using a bell, a buzzer or similar. Once the bell has sounded you must start the course within a designated time, usually 30–45 seconds. The time is set by the association under whose rules you are competing, so check your rule book.

It is *very* important not to pass between the start or finish flags in either direction before the start bell rings. If you start jumping the course before the start bell is rung, you will be eliminated. If you pass through the flags after the bell has rung you will be deemed to have started the course, so be careful if you are circling your horse to settle it after the bell. If you pass through the flags in the wrong direction you may be eliminated.

TIP: In certain circumstances, such as when a competition is held indoors and space is limited, it may be acceptable to pass through the start/finish flags in the wrong direction after the bell in order to start the course. Check with the judge before you start.

Riding the course

Course riding technique

The key to riding a successful showjumping round is to ensure your horse always leaves the ground (takes off) from the correct position in front of the fence (jump). This 'simple' requirement takes a lifetime to perfect.

In *very* simple terms, to successfully negotiate a fence, the horse has to leave the ground at a distance which is slightly greater than the height of the jump. For example, if the fence is 1 m high the horse needs to take off about 1.1–1.7 m in front of the fence, depending on the type of fence. If the horse leaves the ground too far from the fence it may hit the fence on the way down or land on top of the fence. If the horse leaves the ground too close to the fence it may hit the fence on the way up or stop in front of (refuse) the fence.

When a horse is cantering its stride is approximately 3.5 m – the distance from where its feet leave the ground to the point where its feet land again is 3.5 m. Obviously, a horse can only begin to jump a fence by pushing off from the ground – if the correct take-off point for your fence is in the middle of your horse's canter stride you are going to be in trouble! By the time your horse lands you will be too close to the jump.

Top riders can visualise and feel the exact spot in front of the jump where they need to take off from. This is called 'seeing a correct distance'. They adjust the length of their horse's canter stride some distance from the jump to ensure that its stride finishes on the correct take-off point. If they will be too far from the jump they make the horse take bigger strides to get closer to the fence. If they will be too close to the fence they collect the horse to make it take shorter strides.

For less-experienced riders, establishing the correct rhythm (regularity of speed) and tempo (speed) gives the best chance of hitting the correct take-off point. If you allow your horse to go at a regular speed it usually tries to adjust its length of stride to reach the correct take-off point. It is common to see inexperienced riders speeding up as they get closer to the jump. Making your horse go faster in front of a jump will not make it jump better, and you may end up with a horse who learns to speed up at each jump (rush the fences) even when you don't ask it to.

As with cross-country jumping, keep the *Red* flag on your *Right*-hand side as you jump the fence.

A number and a letter on a fence, for example 4a, 4b and 4c, shows a combination fence – the distance between these fences is set out in a very specific way. When you walk the course, ask your instructor or a more experienced rider to tell you how to 'step out' the fence.

Counting the number of steps between two fences lets you work out how many canter strides your horse should do between the combination jumps. Generally, a horse will land two adult strides from the base of a jump, cover four adult strides in each canter stride and take off one adult stride before the next jump. For example, if you step seven adult strides between two jumps it is expected that a horse will take one canter stride between the two jumps (2 + 4 + 1).

Stepping out the course is very important for experienced riders, as they can adjust the length of their horse's stride to fit correctly between the jumps. If you are less experienced, don't worry about trying to remember the distances between fences. If you ride in a good rhythm and tempo, the distances between the fences will work themselves out.

Aim to jump at the centre of the jump, and ensure the horse's nose-to-tail line is at right angles (straight on) to the jump when you take off and land. More experienced riders may jump fences on an angle to reduce their time, particularly in a jumping competition where the fastest time wins. Jumping a fence on an angle increases its difficulty, however, and you are more likely to knock it down.

At the lower levels of pony club or riding club you may even be able to trot around the course and still be within the optimum time. As a trot stride is a lot shorter than a canter stride, you are more likely to hit the correct take-off point. At all other levels of showjumping you will need to canter around the course to avoid time penalties.

Course riding process

In most jumping events you will be required to jump the fences in numerical order. There are different penalties, depending on the class:

- refusing a fence (e.g. your horse stops in front of the fence)
- knocking down a fence, or putting a foot in a water jump
- taking longer than the optimum time.

TIP: The sound of a horse's hoofs hitting the water brings a smile to an eventing rider's face. A showjumping rider is horrified at the sound. In showjumping, the horse must jump over the water without touching it. Water jumps are rarely used except at very high levels of competition.

You can be eliminated for:

- falling off your horse
- jumping the fences in the wrong order (except in specific points/take-your-own-line classes)

A showjumping water jump. The far side is edged with plasticine to help the judge determine whether a horse has incurred a penalty. Photo: Julie Wilson Photography

- starting before the bell is rung
- leaving the arena before going through the finish flags
- exceeding the time limit.

In a showjumping class there is no limit on the number of fences you can knock down. You will of course get lots of penalties, but you won't be eliminated even if you knock down every fence on the course!

Riders often refer to knocking down a fence as 'knocking a rail' or 'having a rail down'. It makes no difference whether you knock down only the top rail or flatten the entire fence. There is the same number of penalties for both. If you knock down a fence, don't worry – just keep going.

If your horse refuses to jump a fence, you must turn around and try again. Make sure you give your horse enough of a run-up, without going so far away that you incur too many time penalties. The clock continues to run when you have a refusal, so don't waste too much time. If you have three refusals over the entire course you will be eliminated, except in special points/speed classes.

If your horse slides to a stop in front of a fence, its front legs may knock the fence down without actually jumping it. The judge will ring the bell to stop the timing clock. The jump will be put back up, the bell will be rung again, the clock restarted and you can try to jump the fence again. You would only receive a penalty for the refusal. You would not be penalised for the knock-down as well.

> **TIP:** An important difference between cross-country and showjumping concerns the riding of combination jumps. In showjumping, a combination fence must be jumped as a combination. If you have a refusal at one part of a combination fence you must jump the entire combination again, for example, if your horse refuses 4b you must jump 4a and 4b again. It is often easier to jump the whole combination again anyway, as the fences are often too close together to get enough rhythm to jump only one part of the combination.

Finishing the course

The end of the course is marked by a red and white flag and a sign saying 'Finish'. You must go between the red and white flag in the correct direction to finish the course – *Red* on your *Right*.

Scores and prizes

The judges will record scores as you ride your course. Depending on the type of showjumping class, you may be required to do a jump-off, either at the end of the class or immediately after your first round. It is up to you to know whether you have made it into the jump-off. In most classes the judge reads a list of riders who are eligible for the jump-off, and the order they will ride in. Make sure you are ready to ride as they will not wait for you to get organised. In stand-alone showjumping (not part of a horse trials event) it is unusual for results to be written on a scoreboard, except at the major showjumping events. In some instances times in jump-offs and speed classes are written on the scoreboard, which is usually near the jumping arena.

In most cases the presentation takes place immediately after the final rider has completed the course. The presentation is most often mounted – you are on your horse. If it is an official competition and you have earned points, you will need to give your card to the judge (if they don't already have it). The judge will fill in the points and sign the card.

What to wear

EFA/FEI

- White, off-white or beige jodhpurs/breeches
- Riding jacket (hacking jacket)
- Shirt and tie *or* shirt and stock *or* rat-catcher collar
- Australian Standards approved helmets must be worn by all riders at all levels, depending on the organising committee's insurance. Check the program
- Long black or brown riding boots (top boots). The boots do not have to be leather – synthetic top boots are fine – *or* leather leggings with matching leather boots *or* short jodhpur boots for juniors

- If the weather exceeds 28°C riders may be allowed to compete without their jacket or, in some instances, in a polo shirt. Check the rule book for details.

Riding club
- Riding club uniform.

Pony club
- Pony club uniform.

Equipment

Always check the rule book for specific saddlery requirements. The information below is only a general guide.

EFA/FEI
The rules regarding equipment in showjumping are fairly relaxed at EFA/FEI level. All saddles/bridles/bits and other equipment are allowed. The only restrictions are:
- Blinkers are not allowed
- Reins must be attached directly to the bit or bridle
- Running reins are not allowed
- Standing martingales must be attached to a conventional cavesson leather noseband
- Long dressage whips are not allowed (75 cm is the maximum length).

Riding club
- Any type of saddle except a sidesaddle, as long as stirrups hang freely from the stirrup bars and are outside the saddle flap
- Any type of bit including gags and hackamores
- Reins must attach directly to the bit or the bridle
- Standing martingales are not allowed
- Blinkers are not allowed
- If saddle only has a single girth strap/girth point a surcingle must be used
- Maximum whip length is 75 cm.

Pony club
- Any type of saddle except a sidesaddle, as long as stirrups hang freely from the stirrup bars and are outside the saddle flap
- Any type of bit excluding hackamores
- Reins must attach directly to the bit or the bridle
- Standing martingales are not allowed
- Blinkers are not allowed

Note the boots on the horse's front legs. The straps across the front are only there to hold the boot in place. The protective part of the boot lies down the back and side of the horse's leg. Photo: Julie Wilson Photography

- If saddle only has a single girth strap/point a surcingle must be used
- Maximum whip length is 75 cm.

> **TIP:** Most showjumping riders put boots on their horse to protect its legs. Showjumping boots are usually open-fronted – the boot covers only the back and sides of the leg – unlike cross-country boots, which wrap all the way around. The open front allows the horse to feel its leg hitting a rail and try to avoid doing it again. Close-fronted boots reduce the horse's sensitivity to hitting rails, so it is less likely to try to avoid them. Showjumping boots are used primarily to protect the tendons which run down the back of the leg.

Where to warm up

You are *never* allowed to warm up in the arena you are going to compete in, on the day of the competition. You may not be allowed to warm up there even the day before, unless the organisers give specific permission to do so.

Showjumping competitions have a practice jump and warm-up area close to the showjumping arena. You are allowed to practise as often as you like, but most horses perform best with just a couple of goes over the practice jumps. The practice jumps have red and white flags to indicate the correct direction for jumping. Make sure you follow the proper course, to avoid colliding with other competitors.

Programs and entries

Whether entries are required in advance or on the day for showjumping competitions depends on the organisers. As a general rule, smaller competitions will accept entries on the day; larger competitions may require entries ahead of time. A discount may be offered if you enter ahead of time rather than on the day. Details of entry requirements are set out in the program or showjumping event handbook.

Handbooks setting out showjumping events can be purchased from each association. Some associations publish a calendar of events on their website. Showjumping events are often run as part of an agricultural show, horse show or gymkhana, and you must contact the relevant committee to get a copy of their event program.

Rules

Each association runs their competitions under their rules. It is essential to have a copy of the correct rule book and read it before you compete. Rules often change and, although the rules across the various associations are fundamentally the same, there are often small differences.

Showjumping summary

Showjumping is an exciting and entertaining sport and the only Olympic equestrian sport where the result doesn't depend on a judge's individual opinion. The showjumping fraternity are an open, supportive and relaxed group who are always happy to welcome newcomers. Go to a showjumping event and give it a go – if you need any help or have a question, just ask the person parked next to you!

6

Before the competition

A month before the competition

Choosing an instructor

To be a successful equestrian competitor, you must have a good riding instructor. Finding the right one can be quite a task. The Equestrian Federation of Australia (EFA) lists accredited coaches on its website, which is a good place to start. The list includes contact details, the coach's level of accreditation and the disciplines which they are accredited to teach. However, there are some excellent instructors who are not accredited with EFA. They can be a little harder to find.

A good way to find the right person is to ask people who are competing successfully at your pony or riding club or at your agistment centre. Someone who is doing well in the competition arena probably has lessons with a good instructor.

Once you have an instructor in mind, arrange a lesson and see what you think. You might need two or three lessons before you can fully assess the instructor. A few criteria for assessing the instructor include:

- whether you felt safe during the lesson. An instructor should never push you to the point of being frightened
- whether you had fun
- whether you learnt something new or improved some part of your riding
- whether the instructor gave you their full attention. An uninterested instructor is a waste of your time and money

- whether you can afford weekly or fortnightly lessons. There is no point going to a very expensive instructor if you can only afford a lesson every couple of months
- whether their facilities are good or whether they are willing to travel to you.

If you can answer 'Yes' to these, you have probably found an instructor who suits you. It is essential to have regular lessons with the same instructor to get any benefit from it. Riders who change instructors constantly, looking for a miracle solution to a riding problem, will be forever disappointed. There is no magic answer. Riding requires consistent and disciplined work.

You owe it to your instructor to do as they say during the lesson, although it is fine to ask a question if you do not understand what they want. You should not question their method – you might be surprised and find it works. If you feel the instructor's methods are not effective, do as you are told for that lesson and don't go back again. There are two very important exceptions to this rule. You have every right to disobey your instructor's directions if you are frightened or if your horse is suffering in any way.

Parents must make sure that their children understand this. Accidents can happen, especially when jumping, if an instructor pushes a frightened child beyond their limits.

TIP: Some riders and parents think that the lessons they receive at a pony/ riding club are all the coaching they need. This is very rarely the case if you want to compete and progress. Although useful, these lessons are often for large groups and usually only once a month. Club instructors are often also available for private lessons.

TIP: A rider's mum, dad, husband, wife or partner are rarely the right choice as an instructor, even if they are wonderful instructors. An arm's-length relationship between instructor and pupil is usually best. It is not unusual for children/spouses of professional instructors to train with someone else, to keep their family relationship separate.

Entries

Requirements vary for different events – some require entries beforehand, by a certain date, and others will accept entry on the day of competition. Get the event program or look it up in the applicable handbook/website and find out the entry requirements. Some associate/pony club/riding club competitions may not appear in the handbook. They are usually advertised in a newsletter or rural newspaper.

Some official pony club competitions require you to enter the competition via your pony club. Either the pony club lodges entry forms for all club members, or the pony club DC (district commissioner) must sign the entry form. Check with your pony club, as entries for these competitions may close earlier than usual.

> **TIP:** Schools competitions generally require a signature from a school representative on the entry form. Get any signatures you need before school holidays.

If entries need to be made ahead of time, do them early! Don't wait until the day before the entries close to send your entry in. The closing date is the latest that the entries can be received by the organising committee, and you must allow plenty of time for postage. Entries for classes in dressage and horse trials may be limited and names are often taken on a first-in first-served basis – the earlier your entry is received, the better your chance of being accepted.

> **TIP:** If you are staying overnight at an event, organise accommodation for you and your horse early. The entry form will advise whether yards/stables are available at the venue and how to book them. If they are not available on-site, the organisers can put you in contact with locals who have stables or yards for hire.

Training plan

Plan how you are going to practise for the competition. Use a diary or a calendar to work out what you are going to practise and when you are going to practise it. For less-experienced riders, it is easy to fall into the trap of practising one facet of riding too much but miss another part – often the part you find hardest and therefore need to practise the most. No matter what discipline you are competing in, you cannot practise every aspect of it every time you ride. The basis for all training should be to focus on one or two parts of your riding each day. Over time, they should come together as a polished performance.

Your training plan should include all aspects of riding leading up to the competition, including your lessons. Your instructor will help you construct a plan. Make sure you stick to it!

Example: for a horse trials competition

- Tuesday 1st: dressage – trot circles, long rein walk and halts on centre line
- Wednesday 2nd: dressage – trot–canter–trot transitions and canter circles
- Thursday 3rd: jumping – arrowheads and straight lines before and after jump
- Friday 4th: jumping – go to pony club grounds and practise water jump and ditches

- Saturday 5th: practice ride through dressage test
- Sunday 6th: riding lesson
- Monday 7th: day off.

Now is the time to start learning your dressage test if you are doing one at the competition. There are many approaches to learning a dressage test, but one of the most effective is to practise the test on foot before you get on your horse. Draw the arena letters onto pieces of paper and lay them on the floor in the correct position. Walk, trot and canter your way through the test. After you have mastered it on the floor you can start riding it on the horse. Some trainers warn riders against riding the test too many times, concerned that it will lead to the horse anticipating the test. I do not agree. It is essential to ride through your entire dressage test at least four or five times before the competition, especially if you are a beginner.

If you are a show rider, make up some workouts and start practising them. Try riding in different areas to improve your ability to pick a marker and centre your workout around it.

It is a good idea to visit a horse event as part of your training plan, whether it is a competition or just a pony club rally. It will familiarise you with how your horse reacts to the atmosphere of competition, and you can use that information to help structure your warm-up plan. Some horses barely raise an eyelid at the line of floats and horses everywhere. Others become a nervous wreck and must be managed carefully. Ride your horse around the venue, and practise riding it near other horses to simulate the often-cramped warm-up areas at competitions.

TIP: All cross-country courses are closed to schooling of horses some time before the actual event. This is usually four weeks – the time is specified in the rule book. No horse or rider is allowed on the course while it is closed. Breaking the rule leads to elimination. If the event will be held at your local club, you need to make arrangements to practise cross-country jumping somewhere else for that time.

If you are competing at a horse trials event, you will need to practise taking your horse into water in preparation for the water jump. The water jump usually causes more difficulties for riders than any other obstacle on the course. Practising a water jump can be difficult, as most are filled only for competitions and remain dry at other times. You do not need a large body of water to practise, nor does the water need to be deep. The only essential is that the base underneath the water be firm, not slippery. Dams are generally a bad choice, as they invariably have a slippery base which will frighten the horse and make it less confident.

If you have a gravel drive or similar, scrape an area 2 m by 3 m and fill it with water to create a puddle a few centimetres deep. Put showjumping rails around the puddle edges and, depending on your competition level, put a small jump on the side you intend to jump from. At lower competition levels you are only required to walk into the water, not to jump over a jump and land in it, so you don't need to practise with a jump. The horse can't judge the water's depth as it's on the far side of the jump – this is why the horse must feel totally confident that you are not going to drown it! Practising in the puddle increases the horse's confidence, so it will be willing to enter the water at the competition.

Shoeing

Now is the time to work out whether your horse will need its feet done prior to the competition. They should be trimmed, or trimmed and shod, roughly every six weeks. If its feet are due to be done prior to the competition, book the farrier to come a week before the event. If its feet are due to be done immediately after the competition, it is still best to get it done the week before rather than risk losing a shoe at the competition.

Avoid getting your horse shod the day before the competition unless absolutely necessary, as some horses' feet can be a little tender for a day or two afterwards.

A week before the competition

Running sheet

By now you should have your start times for the competition, either:

* through the post
* via a website/email
* by ringing a number specified on the program
* via the program which specifies the ring start time, as is most often the case for showing and showjumping.

Check the program or handbook you used when doing your entries, to make sure you know how you will be receiving your times. If you have to ring up for them make sure you do it at the time specified – if you ring outside the allowed hours you may find only an answering machine!

Prepare a running sheet for the day of the competition – a detailed plan of all the tasks that need to be done on the day and who is going to do each task. The running sheet lets your helper (if you have one!) know what is expected of them. This is especially important for inexperienced helpers. If you are on your own, a running sheet helps you stick to your plan even if your nerves start to take over. Hang the completed plan in your car window or float, or tape it to your yard, so everyone in your team knows what is going on. Cross each item off the list after it's completed so you know what has been done.

An example of a running sheet for a horse trials event is shown in Table 6.1.

Table 6.1: Running sheet for Jane, horse trials event

Description	Start time	End time	Person responsible
Feed horse	5 am	5.20 am	Jane
Prepare and load horse onto float	5.30 am	5.45 am	Jane
Drive to event	6 am	7 am	Dad
Unload horse, tie up and get water	7 am	7.15 am	Dad
Report in with card, find dressage arena, get cross-country map and back numbers	7.15 am	7.30 am	Jane
Get horse ready, brush, paint hooves etc.	7.30 am	8 am	Jane
Saddle up horse	8 am	8.15 am	Jane
Change into dressage clothes	8.15 am	8.30 am	Jane
Gear check	8.30 am	8.45 am	Jane
Warm up for dressage test	8.45 am	9.20 am	Jane
Ride dressage test	9.20 am	9.30 am	Jane
Unsaddle horse and give hay and water	9.30 am	10 am	Dad
Walk cross-country course twice	10 am	11.30 am	Jane and Dad
Take hay away from horse	11.30 am	11.30 am	Dad
Put in studs and put on horse's boots	12 pm	12.30 pm	Dad
Saddle up horse	12.30 pm	1 pm	Jane
Change into cross-country clothes	1 pm	1.30 pm	Jane
Gear check	1.45 pm	2 pm	Jane
Take water, sponge etc. to cross-country finish	1.45 pm	2 pm	Dad
Warm-up	2 pm	2.15 pm	Jane
Ride cross-country course	2.15 pm	2.30 pm	Jane
Sponge down and walk horse in vet area	2.30 pm	3 pm	Dad
Unsaddle horse and give water	3 pm	4 pm	Dad
Change into showjumping clothes	3.30 pm	3.45 pm	Jane
Walk showjumping course	3.45 pm	4.15 pm	Jane
Put on horse's showjumping boots	4.15 pm	4.30 pm	Dad
Saddle up horse	4.30 pm	4.45 pm	Jane
Gear check	5 pm	5.15 pm	Jane
Warm-up	5.15 pm	5.30 pm	Jane
Ride showjumping course	5.30 pm	6 pm	Jane
Unsaddle horse and give hay and water	6 pm	6.30 pm	Dad
Thank your helper and buy them a drink			Jane

Equipment list

It is important to have a detailed list of what you need to take to the event. You should start the list early in the week and add to it as you think of new items. After a few competitions your list should be complete and you can use it repeatedly for each event. Gather things you need into a specific area (a spare bedroom is a good spot) as early as possible. Obviously you can't put things such as your saddle into the room until the night before, as you will still be using it, but things such as riding clothes can be put aside early in the week.

Cleaning

If you will wear a riding jacket at the competition make sure you have it drycleaned early in the week, and remember to pick it up!

If you have saddlery that you keep specially for competitions, such as a special bridle, you can clean it early in the week. If you use the same equipment at home and for competitions, still give it a good clean early in the week and then a quick wipe-over the night before the competition.

You will need a clean set of cotton rugs to put on your horse after you wash it. Make sure the rugs that you are going to use are washed and dried well ahead of time.

Horse preparation

Trimming

Some people like to trim their horse's hair a few days before the competition rather than the day before – the adage 'there is only a week between a good and a bad haircut' applies to horses too. Trimmed areas can look a bit rough immediately after they are done, especially when the horse has its winter coat.

To trim your horse for competition you need a set of electric trimming clippers, available from all saddleries and quite reasonably priced. The clippers need to be oiled regularly with sewing-machine oil to remove the hair and dirt. You can trim your horse with scissors, but it is very difficult to get a good result.

Trim your horse's beard (under the jaw) and its whiskers too for showing events. Don't trim the long hairs around its eyes, as these help the horse detect objects and prevent eye injury. Trim the long hair from the fetlocks and any long hair down the back of the legs. Trim a *small* section (roughly 5 cm) of mane at the bottom of the neck (near the wither) and another immediately behind the ears where the bridle passes over the mane. Some show riders don't trim the section of mane behind the horse's ears (the bridle path). They simply part the mane, pushing one section forward between the ears and the other back along the neck.

> **TIP:** The exception to the rule about trimming horses for the show ring is the Shetland pony. Shetland ponies must not be trimmed or plaited – they are always competed with long manes, tails and hairy legs intact.

For showing, you are expected to trim all the hair out of the ears – not an easy task, as most horses aren't keen on this procedure. I believe all horses look better with their ear hair tidied up, even if you are not doing a show. For other disciplines, you can just trim any hair that is sticking out of the ear and around the edges. This is best done with an experienced person who can help if necessary. *Don't* try trimming ears for the first time on your own – once you start there is no turning back! If you do one ear you *have* to do the other. In many cases the horse will have to be twitched to subdue it enough. Twitching involves taking the horse's top lip and squeezing it using a piece of string. Vets and farriers also use this method of subduing a horse.

> **TIP:** Trimming all the hair out of your horse's ears has other consequences beyond looking tidy. The ear hair not only protects the ears from foreign objects, it reduces noise and wind. Flighty horses can react badly to having their ear hair removed. If in doubt, trim your horse's ears a month before the competition and see how it reacts. If the horse is upset about having bald ears don't trim them fully again. It is better to have a horse that has fluffy ears but behaves properly, than a lunatic horse with bald ears.

Trimming in the winter can be a challenge, especially with fluffy ponies or cross-bred horses. The difficulty is knowing where to stop. If you start trimming a fluffy pony's legs you may trim a strip right up to its belly if you're not careful. The same applies with a fluffy chin. To avoid these problems always cut *with* the lie of the hair, for example when trimming legs always start at the top and go down. Don't push the clippers flat against the skin of fluffy horses. Hold the clippers a little away from the leg and move them in closer with each pass. Between passes, step back and check the overview – there is no point clipping your horse's legs bald down the back while the front looks like a mohair jumper. The idea is to get the hair at the back of the horse's leg roughly the same length as that on the front.

Your horse's tail also has to be tidied up. The tail should be cut off squarely at the bottom, and the length depends greatly on your preferred discipline. Current fashion in the show ring requires the horse's tail to be quite short, usually just below the horse's hocks. In other disciplines, most riders cut the tail midway between the hock and fetlock, but this is purely personal preference. Consider how high your horse carries its tail when trimming it. If your horse carries its tail high when moving, as an Arabian does, the tail will appear shorter when it's lifted up so it's a good idea to leave a little extra length.

For the show ring you need to plait or pull your horse's tail. This is acceptable in other disciplines as well, as is leaving the tail natural. A pulled tail means the hair has been removed from either side of the horse's dock; the size of the horse determines how far down the hair is removed. As you can imagine, many horses

A pony after trimming and plaiting. A good trim and neat plaiting can totally transform a horse's appearance. Take the time to present your horse well.

do not take kindly to having the hair pulled out of the side of their tails, and many riders use clippers to achieve the 'pulled' look. The golden rule of clipping a horse's tail is to *never* clip the centre of the tail. Only ever clip down the sides. When standing directly behind the horse you shouldn't be able to see any of the clipped hair – the tail should simply appear narrower. A tail which is clipped in the middle as well as the sides looks like a donkey's tail, and looks like a toilet brush when it is growing out.

Think carefully about whether to pull or clip your horse's tail. It takes approximately four years for a horse's tail hair to grow to full length, and while regrowing it will look dreadful for a time. The safest bet is to plait your horse's tail. It may be more time-consuming but it is a lot easier to repair a plaiting mistake than to repair a clipping mistake.

Pulling the mane
If your horse's mane is too long or thick it will be very difficult to plait, and you will end up with plaits that look like golf balls. Pulling a horse's mane is a slow process and requires practice. It is very important to pull hair out by the roots rather than break it. Not many horses like having their mane pulled!

Many prefer a method which is kinder on the horse and less stressful for the owner. Saddleries sell a special pulling comb with a built-in blade operated via a button on the handle. The comb allows you to cut the mane close to the horse's neck without leaving the bare patches that scissors can cause. No matter how tempting, *never* cut your horse's mane with scissors.

Start at one end of the neck. Take a piece of mane about 3 cm wide (measured where it comes out of the neck) and hold it in your left hand towards the bottom of the mane. Holding your comb or cutting comb in your right hand, push the mane up towards the horse's neck as you would do if teasing a person's hair. With each push upwards you will have less and less mane in your left hand and a bird's nest of hair teased up near the horse's neck.

If you are using a cutting comb, when you have 20 or so hairs remaining in your left hand, push the cutting comb as close to the horse's neck as you can and press the cutting button. The horse will probably be willing to stand still and let you pull its mane with a cutting comb. If the horse's mane has been pulled before with the traditional method, it may tense when it feels you tease up the mane, but will relax soon.

If you are pulling the mane the traditional way with a normal comb, when you have 10–15 hairs remaining in your left hand, hold the hair horizontally from the horse's neck and use the comb to push down sharply on the horizontal hairs. By using the comb in a downwards motion against the taut mane, the hairs will come out at the root. Check to see that there are white roots at the end of the pulled mane. Pull out only a small number of hairs each time. If you try to pull out too many you can't do it in one quick motion, which is not fair on the horse.

Comb out the teased section of hair and repeat the process. Depending on the thickness of the mane you may have to repeat the process several times on each section. It is best to do each section once then move to the next section. Your aim is a mane of medium thickness, about 10 cm long. Keep the mane neat and tidy by pulling it a little every couple of weeks.

Try a few practice plaits to see if the mane is short and thin enough. If the plaits still look like golf balls you must pull the mane again.

TIP: When tackling an unruly mane for the first time, don't pull it to the exact length/thickness that you want section by section. Always move along the neck until you reach the end then return to the start, shortening and thinning a little more with each pass. If you complete one section entirely your horse may be unwilling to remain still, and will toss its head around to make the job impossible. If one section is completed and the rest is untouched the mane will be very uneven and probably look worse than before. If you move along the mane and the horse becomes unsettled, at least the mane will be even and you can continue pulling another time.

The day before the competition

Washing your horse

I doubt any equestrian competitor would list 'horse washing' as their favourite job, but it must be done if you wish to ride competitively. Good washing facilities can make the job a lot easier. The ideal is an undercover concrete or rubber surface with hot and cold running water. The vast majority of riders do not have this sort of facility, but there are ways to make washing easier.

Horses do not enjoy being washed, primarily because they don't like getting cold. On warm days the horse is usually more agreeable to being washed. Horses have a much shorter coat during summer, which also makes washing them much easier. During the cold winter months, when horses are very hairy, they will not think that being washed is a great idea.

Your first step is to dress for the occasion. Gumboots are a must and waterproof pants are very handy. Wear a short-sleeved top even on cold days as a long-sleeved top will quickly become saturated, especially if you are washing a tall horse that you have to reach up to – the water will run back down your arms.

Most horses will have to be tied up (unless they pull back and run away when tied up), so you need somewhere you can tie them safely. Tying your horse to a fence is not a good idea unless the fence is a post-and-rail type. A horse can become very unsettled when it is being washed, moving around and pawing (digging) with its front legs. In this unsettled state it can easily become tangled in a wire fence. If possible, find somewhere sheltered from the wind with a surface that will not turn to mud as soon as you start washing.

> **TIP:** Never tie your horse to a gate or any other object that is not completely solid or immovable. If a horse panics and tries to pull away when tied up (pulls back) and the object to which it is tied also moves, the horse will panic more. Never tie a horse directly to an object (fence, float etc.). Always tie a piece of hay twine (the string used to secure hay bales) to the object then tie the horse to the hay twine. The hay twine is strong enough to stop the horse breaking free under normal circumstances, but it will break and free the horse if it panics. It is better for a panicking horse to be free than tied up. Seeing a horse panic while tied up is terrifying and potentially dangerous – often the horse falls over or becomes tangled in the object to which it is tied. Trying to free a flailing horse from the entanglement can be very dangerous.

Hot water, even in a bucket, is worth using in colder months. Put about ¼ cup of shampoo into a 10 L bucket of warm water. You do not need special horse shampoo for washing its body (although some riders argue that they do a better job) – any human shampoo is fine. You *must* use baby shampoo, which is designed to be gentle on eyes, to wash a horse's face. Its eyes can be damaged over the long term if normal shampoo gets into them.

Wash the horse's tail first – dip it into the bucket and scrub it with your hands then rinse it with clean water. You may have to do this a few times to get it clean. Put some conditioner on the tail and let it soak while you wash the rest of the horse. After you have finished washing the horse, use a hose to rinse the conditioner out of the tail.

Wash the horse's legs next, using a sponge or soft brush dipped into the bucket. The horse will be more settled if you start with the extremities, as it will not be cold. Next wash the head, using the baby shampoo. Be careful not to get water inside the horse's ears, as it will not be impressed! Finally, shampoo the rest of the body. Soap the horse all over then rinse it off. Use a hose, then pour a couple of buckets of warm water over the horse to warm it up at the end. Make sure you rinse all the shampoo off.

A horse with a fluffy coat will need a really good scrub with your hands, especially if it is grey or white. When washing a grey horse, make sure you clean right down to the skin as any dirt left in the hair will rise to the surface and reappear when the horse is dry. Many riders have washed a grey horse only to find an hour later that dirt is back on the ends of the hair. You can get away with less-thorough washing on a dark-coloured horse.

Never use conditioner on a horse's coat or mane. Conditioner will make the coat and mane fluffy, not a preferred 'look' (think sleek jaguar, not fluffy kitten).

TIP: It is easier to get a grey or white horse clean with a special grey-horse shampoo. These shampoos are often purple and are terrific at removing the stains that show up on greys.

TIP: When washing a grey horse, make sure you scrub right under its stomach and rinse thoroughly. If you don't wash and rinse the stomach well, there will be a dirty water mark along its side.

When you have finished washing, scrape the horse down with a sweat scraper (which is never actually used to scrape sweat). There are lots of different and inexpensive sweat scrapers, all of which remove the bulk of the water from the horse's coat. Start at the top of the horse's neck and scrape the water off from top to bottom, as if scraping water off a car windscreen. Dry the horse as best you can with towels, concentrating on the back and rump.

Just like a dog, a wet horse likes nothing better than rolling on the ground, and the dustier the ground the better. If you don't have a stable or a yard with clean bedding, the horse must be completely dry before you put it in the paddock. If the weather is warm you don't need to rug a wet horse immediately. Take the horse for a walk and let the sun dry it. In cold weather you will need to rug it straight away. This is best done by placing dry towels against the horse's coat then putting clean warm rugs over the top. You will need to hold the horse or tie it up where it can't roll, until it is completely dry. Once dry, remove the towels and put the horse in the paddock. If you forget to remove the towels they will slide out from under the rug and frighten your horse.

> **TIP:** Some wet horses will do anything to roll, even when they are tied up. Tie the horse on a surface that is unattractive to roll on, such as concrete or gravel. Ensure that it is tied with a short lead rope in a safe location, for example not to a wire fence. If the lead is long and the surface is attractive the horse may try to roll while tied up, and become entangled.

> **TIP:** Wash your horse straight after you have ridden it. Its warm body will make the cool wash more enjoyable and will also help it to dry faster.

Plaiting your horse

Mane

Plait your horse on the day of the competition or the night before, depending on how early you need to leave. For showing classes, where the plait quality is judged, it is best to plait on the morning of the competition. Plaiting the night before is fine for other disciplines, as long as the plaits are not too tight. Plaiting for showjumping competitions is not required but is preferred at bigger events.

Practice makes perfect. Don't wait until the night before the competition to have your first try at plaiting. Start practising a couple of weeks ahead of time, and you will quickly improve.

The aim is a series of equally sized, equally spaced, neat plaits sitting slightly off to the right side of the horse's neck. The size and space of the plaits depend on how evenly you pulled your horse's mane. Plaits are usually a little thicker in the middle of the neck and smaller at the base, where the mane may be rubbed out by the rug.

Make sure you have all the equipment you need before you start the job:

- bucket, step or ladder (depending on the size of your horse)
- plaiting bands – small elastic bands in various colours to match the mane
- plaiting cotton – available in various colours to match the mane
- a thick blunt darning needle, from a haberdashery. The plaiting cotton often comes with a needle but this may be too small and sharp to work with easily, and cause bleeding fingertips!
- a fine comb for human hair, *not* a horse mane comb with broad teeth

- commercial plaiting spray from a saddlery. You can use human hair control products such as hairspray but horse products are best as they control the hair without making it too slippery or sticky to plait
- scissors.

Always stand on the horse's *right* side (off side) to start plaiting. The job is much easier if you can look down on the horse's neck while working, and you will probably need a step ladder. If you are inexperienced, it is best to divide the hair into equal bunches before you start to plait. As you get more experienced you can skip this step.

Starting at the top of the horse's neck, use the comb to part the hair in a straight line across the neck to create a bunch of mane roughly 5–8 cm wide. Place a plaiting band around the bunch and secure loosely. Continue to part the mane and create bunches along the length of the neck. You may have to redo some bunches towards the base of the neck to achieve a relatively even spacing.

> **TIP:** When showing/hacking make sure the parts between the plaits are very straight and very clean. Judges will inspect the horse's mane in turnout classes and look for dirt or flakes of skin. Give the mane a really good wash, right down to the skin, before you start plaiting.

Using a commercial spray or water, dampen the first bunch of hair and remove the plaiting band. Divide the bunch into three even pieces and start to plait. Try to keep the plait towards the centre of the horse's neck. You will have to plait upwards initially, or you will end with the plait too low down the right-hand side of the neck. Keep the plait tight. When you are near the bottom of the hair, wind the last section of hair around the bottom of the plait and secure firmly with a plaiting band. Repeat this process with each bunch of hair.

> **TIP:** If you have a horse with an extremely thick mane, such as a Clydesdale cross, pulling and plaiting can be difficult. If you are not showing/hacking you may adopt the 'sunbeam' plait – 'hog' your horse's mane. Hogging involves clipping off the entire mane except for the forelock. A hogged mane is perfectly acceptable in all disciplines except showing.

Thread the needle with a piece of cotton about 30 cm long and tie a knot in the end. Push the needle through the end of the plait with the band, and pull the thread through until the band is holding the knot in the cotton. Fold the plait underneath, then pass the needle through the base of the plait where it joins the neck – be careful not to prick your horse's neck. Pull the cotton through so that the bottom of the plait is pulled up against the base of the plait in a big loop. Pass the needle back through the base of the plait and push it through the bottom of the

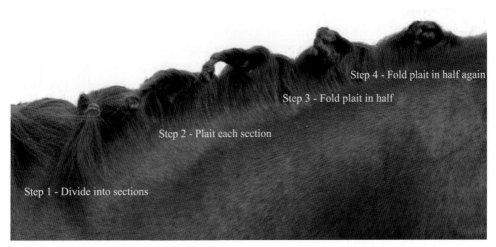

Step 4 - Fold plait in half again

Step 3 - Fold plait in half

Step 2 - Plait each section

Step 1 - Divide into sections

Stages of plaiting the horse's mane.

loop you created. Pass the needle through the base of the plait again. In effect, you have folded the plait in half, then in half again. The second fold of the plait won't resemble a loop. It will look more like a ball. Pass the thread back and forth through the ball until it is held tight, and cut the thread off close to the plait. There is no need to tie a knot in the thread as it will be secured by its passes through the final plaited ball.

> **TIP:** Always start plaiting at the top of the neck. As the horse becomes bored or unsettled, it may start to move its head around. Even a slight movement can make plaiting difficult at the top of the neck. The base of the neck is less affected by head movement, making plaiting easier.

Tail and forelock

The horse's tail has to be plaited (braided) or pulled for showing. In other disciplines the choice is yours, and an increasing number of riders leave the tail in its natural state. Make sure you scrub the tail right down to the skin to remove any flaking skin and dirt.

To plait a tail, the hair is pulled in from either side of the dock (tail bone) into a plait down the centre of the dock. Pulling the outside hairs across to the centre of the dock creates the impression that the horse's tail is narrow at the top. The aim is a straight neat braid down the centre of the dock, and the finer the plait the better. The length of plait depends on the horse, but halfway down the dock is usual.

Getting the braid right takes a lot of practice, so practise before the event. Starting at the top of the tail, take a few hairs from the very edge of the dock where the tail starts growing (the horse's tail only grows on the top and side of the dock, the underside of the dock is skin). The first piece is right at the top of the dock and virtually underneath it. Taking a piece from each side, pull them into the very centre of the tail and cross them over twice so they are in effect twisted together. Holding the twist *very* tightly, take another piece of hair from the side of the dock and pull it into the centre to form the third piece of braid. Always take the third piece from the side of the tail not from the centre.

With each plait, pick up another piece of hair from the edge of the dock and pull it into the centre plait, using the same technique as braiding a person's hair. A common problem is that the plait gets thicker as you progress down the tail. This is caused by taking overly big pieces of hair. Keep the pieces of hair small and aim to have them lying horizontally across the horse's dock. If the pieces start to angle down in a V shape towards the plait, they are either too big or you are not holding the plait tightly enough.

Don't try to bring all the hair from the edge of the dock into the plait, or the plait will be far too thick. When selecting the piece to pull in, leave a small gap between it and the previous piece. The hair left in the gap will lie flat down the tail and be held in place by the pieces lying across it. The hair being pulled in from the sides should resemble a tiny ladder running up either side of the plait.

Secure the end of the braid with an elastic band, leaving a bunch of hair lying down the horse's tail. Alternatively, continue to plait from the end of the braid without pulling in hair from either side. Secure the end of the plait with a plaiting band and fold the plait under itself to form a loop. Secure it with a separate plaiting band at the base of the braid.

The forelock should be braided using the same technique as the tail. At the end of the forelock braid, continue the plait to the very end of the hair and secure with a plaiting band. Fold the plait under in a loop and pass the end up the centre of the braid. To pass the plait through the braid, push your finger up through the braid to make a hole or, for a more professional finish, use a large darning needle or crochet hook to pull the end of the plait through without disturbing the braid. Pull the plait through the braid as far as you can. Ideally, you should not be able to see a loop at the bottom of the braid.

If your braid is very tight you won't need to secure the loop. However, if there is any chance of the plait slipping out from the braid, put a plaiting band around the loop to form a small ball similar to the plaits on your horse's neck, or stitch the loop in with some plaiting cotton.

TIP: Plaiting a horse which is moving around is very difficult. If your horse tends to be unsettled, plait it at home where it is most comfortable rather than at the competition where there will be lots of distraction. Even if your horse is very quiet, plaiting it at home means that you won't panic to get it done at the event.

TIP: Take great care when plaiting or pulling a horse's tail. Some people place a hay bale or stable door between themselves and the horse to reduce the risk of being kicked.

Cleaning your gear

Your saddlery will need a good clean before the competition. Leather gear will require leather cleaner and a leather cream, a synthetic saddle needs only a cloth and water.

Either soap or liquid leather cleaners are fine. When using a saddle soap, you must lather the soap onto a damp cloth then use that cloth on your saddle. If you rub the soap directly onto the saddle it will get stuck in the stitching.

Use plenty of old cleaning rags and rub hard, especially when showing as the judge will inspect your equipment carefully. Pay special attention to folded pieces of leather, such as stirrup leathers where the stirrup sits and bridle cheek straps where the bit sits. Folded leather gets very dirty, and show judges check these folds in turnout classes.

Once you have cleaned the leather, use a leather cream to keep it soft and protected. There is no need to use saddle oil on a bridle unless it is brand new (when it will need to be oiled several times). Modern saddles do not need any oil and are best treated with leather cream from the outset. An oil-soaked bridle or saddle will stretch, become misshapen and attract the dirt.

While cleaning your tack, check for signs of dangerous wear. Pay special attention to folded leather such as the bridle cheek strap where it attaches to the bit and the girth points. Any areas with cracks or tears should be inspected by a saddler and repaired or replaced.

TIP: To clean a bridle or saddle properly you must undo all the buckles and lay the leather down flat. Before you undo anything write down the hole number for each buckle on the bridle and stirrup leathers, for example 'noseband 3 holes from top'. You don't want to saddle your horse at the competition and find that your bridle is now the wrong size.

The easiest way to clean bits and stirrups is to let them soak in a bucket of water. After half an hour you should be able to wipe them clean. Special bit cleaners add a bit of shine but *cannot* be used on the mouthpiece.

All bits have a front and back and many have a top and bottom. Knowing which way the bit goes is not always easy. Be very careful when assembling the bridle and make sure you get the bit the right way around. Your instructor or saddlery will show you which way the bit should go, and teach you how to recognise the correct way.

Clean your boots and spurs and wipe over your helmet too.

Confining your horse

Most experienced competitors keep their horse in a stable the night before a competition. A stable not only keeps the horse clean, dry and safe, but allows a fast getaway when you have an early start. If you don't have a stable, there are a number of suitable alternatives.

If there is a shelter shed in your paddock, you or a friendly handyperson can attach a horse-safe gate (with only small holes that a horse cannot get its hoofs through) or a timber rail to confine the horse. A shelter shed filled with straw makes a great alternative to a stable.

> **TIP:** Some horses, and most ponies, will eat their bed of fresh straw. Such horses should be bedded down on sawdust/rice hulls or shavings. These can be purchased by the truckload if you intend to confine your horse often, or in wool packs from a feed store.

If you have the use of a small yard (approx. 4 m by 4 m), it can be filled with straw for the night to keep your horse cleaner than out in the paddock. A yard must be made of posts with timber or synthetic rails. *Do not* put your horse in a yard fenced with wire or electric tape, as it is highly dangerous. Correctly built electric tape and wire fences are acceptable paddock fencing but are not suitable for yard construction.

If you do not have access to a stable or a yard, use the cleanest paddock available and make sure you have a torch. Horses can be very difficult to find on a dark morning!

It is *essential* to practise confining your horse before the competition to see how it reacts. Never make your first try the night before a competition. Separation anxiety is very common in horses and although some horses don't mind being locked in a stable on their own, others have a complete nervous breakdown and spend the night whinnying and walking in circles. If your horse gets upset at being alone in a stable or yard, put a friend in an adjacent stable/yard to keep it company.

Most horses become used to confinement, but if your horse is very unsettled even with a friend just leave it in the paddock and allow time in the morning to clean off any mud.

Packing

If you are travelling to the competition by float, connect the float and check the lights are working correctly the night before. Go through your checklist and pack everything you need into the car and float. You still need to pack even if you are riding to the competition – fill a backpack with all your bits and pieces. If someone else is driving your car and meeting you there, make sure everything from your checklist is in the car.

TIP: Tick items off your checklist as they go into the car. Not when you pick them up. Not when you take them to the back door. Tick them when you put them in the car.

TIP: Fill the car with petrol the day before. You don't want to be driving around, with a horse float, looking for a petrol station that is open at 5am.

If there are items that cannot be packed until the morning, such as a hay net, put the checklist on the dashboard and make sure you tick off the last items in the morning – *including* your horse. This is not as silly as it sounds. People have been known to arrive at competitions with everything except their most important piece of equipment – their horse!

If you stay overnight at a competition you may be short of storage space in the car and need to pack supplies in the float. If your float has a separate storage compartment, you can fill it to the rafters. However, if you intend to pack items such as hay in the horse section of the float you will need to be very careful. It is surprising how far a hay bale can move in the back of a float. Secure it well – it must not be able to slide under the horse.

TIP: When your horse has to go, he has to go. It happens inside a float as easily as in a paddock. Horse poo is not a problem and is easily cleaned up. Horse pee, on the other hand, makes a big mess. Any gear packed in with your horse may end up wet and smelly. A pile of sawdust/shavings under the horse will help absorb and confine any mess.

The day of the competition

Travelling to the competition

Follow your running sheet strictly, and always allow extra time in case something goes wrong. You are probably going to be nervous, so don't add to the pressure by leaving yourself short of time. If you are relying on a driver to get up and take you, wake them early so they have time to get ready.

Know exactly where you are going. Simply knowing which town the event is in is not enough – you must know where in the town. Some programs include specific directions; if not, ring the organising committee beforehand for clear directions.

Show and pony club grounds are often adjacent to the racecourse in country towns, and in most cases the racecourse is signposted. If you are lost, head for the

The correct way to tie a horse and hay net.

racecourse and you may find your competition. If not, there will usually be people around who can give you directions.

When you arrive, find a suitable parking spot and follow your plan. Your first priority is to make sure your horse is safe and secure. Always tie up your horse with the rope short enough to prevent it reaching below the top of the wheel arches on your float (or the equivalent height in a yard). If the horse is tied with a long rope it may get entangled in the rope and injure itself. When tying up a hay net, make sure it is high so that the horse can't get its hoof stuck in it.

Rider essentials

Nerves

Nerves are a natural part of competing. Top riders use the rush of adrenaline to fire them up to perform at their peak. In less-experienced riders, nerves can have a detrimental impact on performance by causing them to lose focus. You can reduce the negative impact by sticking doggedly to the strict plan that will keep you feeling in control.

Adrenaline prepares your body for 'fight-or-flight', and one way your body does this is by getting rid of any waste. This means lots of trips to the toilet! This is perfectly normal and everyone is affected similarly. The portable toilet at the start of a cross-country course is there for this reason, and it gets a good workout.

> **TIP:** Don't watch! If you get nervous, avoid watching competitors before you have competed yourself. Watching others compete can increase your nervousness if you start thinking 'I hope I don't make that mistake' or 'I won't be able to beat that horse'. As you have no control over your competitors, just ignore them. Focus on what you can control – your horse and your riding.

Whether you socialise at the event before you ride depends on your personality. Some riders find that being a social butterfly before they compete makes them even more nervous. If this applies to you, sit quietly in your float during any free time and go over your riding plan/dressage test/jumping course. If you sit with your back to the float ramp, visitors are unlikely to intrude.

If chatting to friends helps you relax then by all means do so, but make sure you stick to your timetable.

> **TIP:** Some riders take their horse for a walk and let them pick the grass when they arrive, to help calm their nerves and give the horse an opportunity to settle into the atmosphere.

Helping the nervous rider

Helping a nervous rider is the toughest job at the event. Nerves can manifest in lots of different ways:

- tears
- anger
- fear.

Ultimately it is up to the rider to manage their nerves, but you can certainly help.

Following the running sheet to the letter will reduce the rider's stress levels. If you get waylaid by people wanting to chat, excuse yourself and get back to your job.

Don't talk too much to the rider unless they want to, and don't discuss other competitors' performances. The last thing a rider needs is for their helper to come back from the scoreboard with a report such as 'Jane got a really low score, the test must be really hard'. Simply ask the rider 'Do you want me to do anything for you?' then leave them alone.

If you are helping a very nervous rider you will need the patience of a saint – you may be on the receiving end of a short temper. Competing does not excuse bad behaviour, but do your best to let the odd misdemeanour slide without comment.

Eating and drinking

Nervous riders may find it difficult to eat or drink before they compete. However, you *must* eat and drink. I cannot emphasise this enough. A rider who does not eat and drink will become weak, distracted and ineffective in their riding, which not only degrades their performance but may lead to accidents. The impact of dehydration and inadequate diet on the athlete's body is well documented.

Imitating a horse is a good way to get food and water into your body – graze! Small amounts of food and water, often, are the key. Eat good food that will provide sustained energy, not a short sharp sugar hit. Don't expect the food you want to be available at the venue. Most canteens have a fairly limited selection, so always pack your own snacks such as:

- wholegrain cereal
- wholegrain sandwiches
- handfuls of nuts and dried fruit
- fruit, particularly bananas and apples
- muesli bars
- plain water
- sports drinks.

When you are competing you should avoid:

- soft drinks, especially those with caffeine
- chocolate and sugary lollies
- pies and chips. These are best left until after you have finished competing, or your nerves may make them return from whence they came.

Warming up

Knowing your horse well is essential in developing a warm-up routine, and over time you will get to know what routine best suits your horse. Work with your instructor and *write down* your plan. If nerves kick in on the day you may not be able to remember your plan – have it documented.

Your horse must be given rest during the competition. When you have finished your class take the horse back to your float or yard and unsaddle it. Make sure it has access to clean water when you are not riding and that it can nibble some hay.

The excitable horse

Leave plenty of time in your running sheet to warm up or, probably more correctly, calm down an excited horse. A horse that is excitable at home will be worse at the competition. Even a relatively calm horse may get overly excited. This is especially true among ex-racehorses, which associate the large numbers of horses and floats with a trip to the racetrack.

A lunge is often a good way to start if the horse is very upset or you are concerned about what it might do. Saddle up as if you were going to ride, including the bridle. Get yourself dressed and ready to ride too, including helmet, boots and gloves.

Secure the reins around the horse's neck by unbuckling them, wrapping them around twice and doing up the buckle. If you have a lunging cavesson (a head collar used to lunge horses) put it on over the top of your bridle. If you don't have a lunging cavesson, pass the lunging rein through the horse's bit then through the noseband and clip the lunging rein onto itself. If you clip the lunging rein directly to the bit, the bit can pull through the horse's mouth and leave you with little control. Lunging is much more effective if done with side reins or similar. The side reins need not be tight. They simply help keep a horse's mind on the job and stop it looking around too much.

> **TIP:** Side reins can never be used when you are riding a horse and are not allowed for lunging at pony club events.

Your instructor will show you the correct lunging technique and help you fit your side reins or equivalent. Keep any loose lunge rein gathered in your hand, not looped around itself or dangling around your feet.

Once your horse has settled a little on the lunge (10–20 minutes is usual, but all horses are different), remove the lunging gear and climb aboard. In this part of the warm-up all you are concerned with is the basics – walk, trot and canter each way. Your horse may be most settled if it can see the other horses but is not in among other horses warming up.

As it becomes more settled you can move your warm-up a little closer to the area where you will compete. Don't stay on your horse too long, and don't worry if it is not going exactly as you would like. The purpose of this warm-up stage is to take the edge off the horse's excitement.

After 30–40 minutes of riding take the horse back to the float or yard, remove the bridle and tie up the horse. There is no need to remove the saddle. Just loosen the girth a couple of holes to make it comfortable and put a rug over the top if the weather is cold. Give the horse access to water, but don't feed it.

While your horse is resting, complete your own preparations such as doing your hair and putting on your competition clothes. If your horse was still fresh when you got off, you will need to get back on about 40 minutes before you are due to compete. If the horse had calmed down you could remount only 20 minutes before you start. With an excitable horse, it is generally better to be in the saddle a little early rather than a little late.

During the second part of your warm-up you should work through the warm-up routine you planned with your instructor. Stick to the plan. Don't get stuck on one aspect of riding, and remember you are not going to teach the horse anything new during warm-up. If you do have trouble with a specific aspect of riding during the warm-up, it may help to leave it then come back to it later. For example, if you cannot get your horse to canter on the correct leg, don't just keep trying. Have a walk and remember what your instructor said about getting the horse to canter on the correct leg. See if you can work out what is going wrong. Are you leaning forward? Is your horse flexing and bending the right way? Are your legs in the correct position? After thinking it through and trying something different, you might solve your problem.

If you are riding in more than one class at the event, your horse will need less and less preparation time for subsequent classes. For example, in eventing 10–15 minutes is ample warm-up prior to cross-country if you have already done a long warm-up prior to the dressage. In the show ring a long warm-up before your first class will probably do, and after that 5 minutes before each class should be enough.

Avoid giving an excitable horse high-energy feeds such as grains or pellets at the competition. Hay is enough. Remove the hay an hour before you ride so the horse is not exercising on a full stomach.

Separation anxiety can play a significant part in a horse's nervous behaviour. Horses can become very attached to each other, especially when they are kept together. It is best to reduce your horse's dependence on another individual horse. A horse needs companionship, but a group of friends is better than a bosom buddy.

If circumstances allow, rotate your horse's paddock or stable arrangements so it is not always adjacent to the same horse. If you have two horses that are very attached and are both going to a competition, be aware of the potential consequences – a day of horses neighing to each other can be very stressful. A competition is not the right place to take your horses out together for the first time, or to separate them for the first time. Take them to the local pony club and see how the horses behave when you take one away from the other.

If you are taking one horse to the competition and leaving its friend at home, the horse which is left behind should be confined if it shows signs of anxiety, to reduce the risk of injury.

The quiet or lazy horse

All horses must be warmed up. Even quiet old ponies need a bit of time to warm up their stiff muscles and joints. For very young riders on quiet ponies, a 10–15 minute walk, trot and canter in both directions is fine. Older riders and less-experienced horses need a bit more structure, but a 30–50 minute warm-up is generally sufficient.

A very lazy horse must be revved up. Your instructor will develop some exercises to get your horse a little more enthusiastic. For example, you may have to ride the horse in a forward-going trot, then a slower trot and back again. Repeating this exercise several times around a circle can help to get your horse going.

Your horse may respond well to an additional feed between classes at the competition, in line with what you would normally feed it at home. The horse needs at least an hour between finishing the feed and being ridden – it is best not to work a horse with a full stomach.

Summary

Preparation of yourself and your horse is critical if you wish to succeed in the competition arena. It may not guarantee a winning performance, but it certainly gives you and your horse the greatest opportunity to perform to the best of your ability. If you leave no stone unturned in preparation you will never walk away from a performance saying 'If only I had …'.

7

Tools of the trade

Choosing a horse

Selecting the right horse is essential for safe and enjoyable equestrian competition. It takes a lot of research and looking around. This chapter sets out some guidelines that will give you a better chance at choosing the right horse.

Choosing a horse is an absolute minefield which makes buying a used car look like a walk in the park. If possible, have an experienced and trusted horse person, preferably your instructor, help you make this important decision.

You will probably go through the selection process several times during your riding career, as the horse that was suitable at the start of your competition career is rarely still the right horse for you in later years. This is true for both adult and child riders – not only may you outgrow your horse physically, but you may also outgrow its ability.

Knowing the rider

Before you start looking for a horse you need to know what sort of rider you are (or your child is). Are you new to horse riding? Are you a competent rider who is moving into the competition arena? Are you a nervous or brave rider? How old are you? How tall are you? What discipline do you want to compete in?

The answers influence the type of horse you choose. If you are new to riding you will need a beginner's horse; if you already ride but are just starting to compete you will need a quiet but not a beginner's horse. If you are a nervous rider you will probably prefer a lazy horse; brave riders will lean towards a horse that is a bit more energetic.

The rider's height and age are factors to consider. Very young riders do not have the coordination and strength of a teenager or adult. Senior riders may lack flexibility and be carrying old injuries that affect their ability to ride and handle certain horses, for example a person with a back injury will need to look for a horse which provides a smooth ride.

Be careful not to overestimate your own ability.

Horse's temperament

The number one criterion for selecting any horse is that it be *safe*. Every other criteria comes a long way second, especially for a child's horse – under no circumstances should you ever knowingly put a child on a dangerous horse. Old cowboy stories of toughening kids by putting them on bucking bush ponies are absolute nonsense. A rider will not only be frightened by a dangerous horse, but can also be seriously hurt.

There is a difference between a *beginner's* horse and a *quiet* horse.

A beginner's horse must be able to cope with everything it meets – these horses are often referred to as 'bomb-proof'. A beginner will make lots of mistakes which the horse must tolerate, such as losing their balance, accidentally pulling on the reins and accidentally kicking the horse on the rump when getting on and off.

If the horse is for a child it must also be able to tolerate children-specific challenges, such as being made to dress up in various costumes, carrying more than one rider at a time, being ridden bareback and carrying anything the rider chooses, including coats, buckets, flags and the family cat. Horses that are this tolerant are generally a little lazy and not overly sensitive to the rider's aids (legs, hands and seat). This is exactly what you want for a beginner's horse. A sensitive, responsive and forward-going horse is completely unsuitable for a beginner, as any involuntary signals from the rider results in a response from the horse. If the beginner rider needs to kick three or four times to get the horse started, that is just fine!

A quiet horse is generally a horse with a desirable temperament (doesn't buck, rear, bolt etc.) that is not upset by changes in its surroundings. A quiet horse is suitable for a rider who is new to competition riding but has general riding experience. A quiet horse will not get overly excited at competitions and should be more responsive to the rider's aids than a beginner's horse is, as the rider will give fewer involuntary signals to the horse. For example, the rider is less likely to lose their balance and accidentally kick the horse.

A horse competing at the Olympics may be very quiet but it will certainly not be a beginner's horse – it will be highly sensitive to the rider's exacting aids.

When choosing a horse, make sure you know whether you need a quiet horse or a beginner's horse. Some riders are willing to take horses with poor

Children's ponies must be very tolerant. Dressing up is just one activity that junior riders inflict on their mounts! Photo: Julie Wilson Photography

temperaments because they also have other desirable traits, for example an experienced rider may put up with a horse that is very excitable because it has an excellent jumping technique. Someone starting out in equestrian sports should avoid any horse that doesn't have a quiet temperament, no matter what other desirable attributes it may have. Learning the skills required to compete in your chosen sport is difficult enough without having to cope with an emotional horse.

> **TIP:** Be careful when buying a horse which is very underweight. It will be unhealthy, just like a very underweight person. It may show a very quiet temperament, due to lethargy – the placid manner may simply be due to malnourishment. Once the horse puts on weight and becomes healthier its temperament may change.

Horse's age

It is common for inexperienced parents to choose a young horse for their young rider, thinking that they will 'grow up and learn together'. This may work when selecting a puppy but it does not apply to horses. As a general rule, horses mellow with age. Younger horses tend to be more excitable and older ones are usually quite laid back. Of course there are always exceptions, but it is helpful to remember this guide: the horse's age and experience should be considered together.

Horses are usually ridden for the first time between two and three years of age. Rarely is a horse of this age suitable for a beginner or inexperienced competition rider. Most horses start to show an adult temperament by about eight and continue to mellow. The competition career of most horses draws to a close in their late teens or early 20s; the retirement age of ponies is closer to 25–30.

It is rare to find a genuine beginner's horse which is under eight – they are much more likely to be in their late teens or older. As horses age beyond about 15 their value decreases, which means there are often great bargains if you are willing to buy an older horse. On the other hand, a very old horse may be difficult if not impossible to resell, so you need to be able to look after it in its retirement. An old experienced horse is worth its weight in gold, even if it costs several thousand dollars without any chance of resale. These horses are often referred to as 'schoolmasters'. The money you spend on them should be considered an investment in your riding, rather than an investment in a horse.

TIP: When viewing young riding horses (<4 yrs) remember that they have not developed their full physical strength. They tire quickly when being ridden – a very young horse can take only 20–30 minutes. Such horses have been ridden only by professional horseriders/breakers and may appear very quiet. As they get older and are taken away from the strictly disciplined environment of professional riders, they may turn out to be less quiet than you thought.

Horse's experience

An untrained horse and an untrained rider are not a good combination. However, it is equally a problem if the horse is too trained for the rider. Competition horses should be viewed as steps on a ladder – you need to go up one step at a time, not from bottom to top in one leap. Very eager (and wealthy) parents or riders have purchased Olympic-level horses for beginner competitors, only to find the highly trained horse impossible to ride.

Horses trained to the highest level are very sensitive to the rider's aids. A less-experienced rider will not have the skills to correctly apply these aids and may give the horse involuntary signals. For example, a Grand Prix dressage horse will respond if the rider's leg is moved forward or back only a few centimetres, as this is what it has been trained to do. A rider starting out is rarely in total control of their leg position (or hands or seat). If they apply involuntary movements to a highly trained dressage horse they might end up going sideways, backwards or spinning in a circle!

As a guide, you should purchase a horse two to three levels above your current capabilities, for example if you are currently competing at Grade 4 pony club, a horse competing at Grade 2 would probably suit you. If you are a Grade 4 pony club rider and you purchase a Grand Prix level horse, you are probably going to be disappointed. Some riders have succeeded by jumping straight to the top of the ladder, but this is the exception rather than the rule.

A horse with documented experience is better than one with hearsay experience. If the seller can show the grading cards, dressage test sheets or ribbons the horse has won, it is proof that the horse has the ability to compete successfully. This is an important factor in making your decision. Be suspicious of someone selling a horse that is 'trained to advanced level' but that has never set foot in a competition arena. Why hasn't it competed? Will it misbehave at a competition? Purchasing the unknown is always a risk.

A horse doesn't have to compete to be a good horse – some horses go to pony club every month but don't compete much. For this type of horse, ask the pony club DC or other members their opinion of the horse. Judging a horse's experience is like judging a person's résumé when they apply for a job – check that the references they give, and the qualifications they say they have, are true!

> **TIP:** Ex-racehorses are readily available in Australasia to be re-trained for the competition arena, and many reach the highest levels of equestrian sport. In general, ex-racehorses which are not yet re-trained for equestrian sports are totally unsuitable for riders starting out in the competition ring. These horses are referred to as being 'off the track'.
>
> A racehorse has been taught only one thing – to run very fast! When you take an ex-racehorse to a competition which has a racecourse atmosphere, it will want to run fast. Re-training for competition riding requires an experienced rider and an extended period, and some such horses will never relax in the competition environment. If you want to purchase an ex-racehorse which has plenty of successful competition experience, do so. If an ex-racehorse is 'schooling well at home' but hasn't been to a competition, don't consider it unless you are very experienced.

Horse's height

Size is an important factor when choosing a horse, especially for children. In some disciplines the size of the horse affects eligibility for competitions, for example a horse must be 14.2hh to compete in official open dressage classes. It is important to know any height rules in your chosen disciplines.

To determine what size horse is right for you, draw an imaginary horizontal line across the horse's belly halfway between the top of its back and the bottom of its stomach. The bottom of the rider's foot should rest on the horse's side below this line but not below the horse's belly.

The horse's height should be viewed as rungs on a ladder, for children. Horses are not school shoes. You cannot buy a horse a couple of sizes too big so that the child will grow into it. Moving a child from a 13.2hh pony to a 16hh horse is a massive jump which may make the child frightened and reluctant to ride. A child is better off being undermounted (riding a horse which is too small) and safe and happy, than overmounted (riding a horse which is too large) and frightened.

Being overmounted or undermounted does not affect judging, except in some turnout or rider classes in the show ring. The horse/rider sizes should not be considered in the judging criteria for horse show classes or in the dressage arena.

The rider's ability to handle the horse on the ground, such as saddling up, leading, putting rugs on etc. is also a consideration when choosing the right height. Everything is a little easier with a smaller horse, whether it is washing them or putting on their rugs. Also consider any physical limitations of the rider – many older riders choose smaller horses as shoulder injuries make it hard for them to reach up to saddle and rug tall horses.

Don't be overly concerned about a horse's height. If the horse and the rider are happy don't hurry to move the rider up to a bigger horse. They will move on when they are ready.

Breeds

The breed is of little consequence for equestrian sports unless you wish to show your horse in a specific breed class. However, some breeds are favoured in each discipline, as they show the traits which are desirable in that specific discipline.

Unlike the dog world, purebred horses are no more valuable than crossbred horses. The breeding list of Olympic horses shows that a significant proportion were crossbred to combine the desirable traits of more than one breed. In simple terms, horse breeds can be split into two groups – hot-blooded and cold-blooded. This has nothing to do with blood. It is a generalised description of a breed's characteristics. Hot-blooded horses tend to be faster and fine-boned. They have better endurance and can be more excitable. Thoroughbreds and Arabian horses are the two most common. Cold-blooded horses were traditionally working horses which were stronger, slower and heavier-boned, with a more placid temperament. They include draft horses, Clydesdales and heavy pony breeds.

Over time the hot- and cold-bloods were mixed to create horses with desirable traits for equestrian competition. In some cases, breeding has gone on for so many generations that the cross-breeding has created a breed in its own right. Common examples include:

- warmbloods – these horses originated in Europe as a result of crossing, primarily, draft horses with thoroughbreds. The resulting horses are defined as breeds in their own right, often distinguished by the geographical region in which the horses were bred, e.g. Holstein, Hanoverians and Dutch warm-bloods

- riding ponies – resulted from breeding thoroughbreds with various traditional pony breeds
- Irish sport horses – increasing in popularity, derived from crossing Irish draft horses with thoroughbreds
- Anglo-Arabians – defined as a cross between an Arabian and a thoroughbred.

In the show ring, thoroughbreds, riding ponies, Welsh ponies, Australian ponies and Shetland ponies are the most common breeds although thoroughbreds crossed with warmbloods are becoming increasingly popular in hunter classes. For dressage, warmbloods and warmbloods crossed with thoroughbreds dominate. Thoroughbreds, Irish sport horses, Clydesdale crosses and various pony breeds are also well represented. The thoroughbred was traditionally the breed of choice for eventing and showjumping riders in Australasia but it is now very common to see Irish sport horses, warmbloods and warmblood–thoroughbred crosses taking on the jumps.

Allying horse breeds with a particular discipline is only a guide to what is most popular in each discipline. There is *no* restriction on what breed of horse you ride, except in specific showing breed classes. There is no reason why you can't do dressage on an Appaloosa and showjumping on a quarterhorse, for example. I know at least one Appaloosa that competed successfully to Grand Prix level dressage.

TIP: Thoroughbred does not mean purebred. A thoroughbred is simply a breed of horse in the same way as a labrador is a breed of dog. Thoroughbreds are the most common breed of horse in Australasia, as huge numbers are bred for the racing industry.

TIP: Horses are often advertised as holding multiple registrations with various breed societies. This is of little consequence unless you intend to breed the horse or compete in specific breed classes. Don't place too much importance on such registrations. It is also common to see a horse promoted as 'EFA-registered'. Registration with EFA is open to any horse or pony, and once a horse is registered with EFA it is registered for life. Buying a horse that is EFA-registered only saves you having to spend a few dollars to register it if you want to compete in official EFA competition. It certainly should not be a factor in your decision.

Viewing and trialling a horse

Unless you know a horse and/or its owner very well, always go to a horse viewing with a degree of suspicion. The term 'buyer beware' could have been coined just for the horse trade! If you are likely to get caught up in the emotion of trying a horse, jot down some questions beforehand and some criteria by which you will assess the horse. At the minimum you should ask:

- what is the horse's age and do you have proof through registration?
- what is the horse's experience, and is it documented?
- has the horse been given any medication in the past month. If yes, what?
- has the horse had any illnesses or injuries that you know of?
- does the horse have any vices such as biting, kicking, bolting, weaving or wind-sucking?
- is it good to shoe, float, clip and tie up?

Be prepared to ride. Bring your helmet, back protector, boots and jodhpurs. Some people like to use their own saddle but this is not always possible as it may not fit the horse. A video camera and cameraperson are also handy, especially if your instructor cannot come with you. A video will let you show them the horse later on.

It is a good idea to arrive 20–30 minutes before your viewing appointment to see whether the horse is being exercised. If the horse is hot or shows signs of being ridden recently, ask the seller why it was ridden. It is very important not to be intimidated by the seller. If you are likely to get intimidated, take someone with a strong personality. The person helping you need not be familiar with horses, they just need to be familiar with someone doing a hard sell!

Safety is always the number one rule. If the horse looks dangerous or shows any undesirable traits such as biting or kicking, turn around and go home. Have a good look at riding facilities. If you are offered a rocky paddock on the side of a hill ask the owner to take the horse to the local pony club grounds so that you can try it out properly.

Always ask the seller to get on the horse first. If the seller isn't willing to ride the horse, you certainly shouldn't. There are always exceptional circumstances where the seller may not have an appropriate rider available. If this is the case, lunge the horse first and ride it in a safe enclosed area. Give the horse a good ride – make sure you walk, trot and canter in both directions. If you want to use the horse for jumping, ride it over a few small practice jumps. If the facilities are suitable, also take the horse out for a ride in a large paddock to see how it reacts.

It is always desirable to ride a horse more than once before you purchase it. Ideally, try to find an opportunity to ride the horse away from its home environment – it may not be possible but it is always worth asking. You may be able to watch the horse at a pony club or competing where, even if you can't ride it, you can get a good idea of how it behaves.

TIP: Taking a horse for a trial period prior to purchase is fraught with danger. The problem is that accidents do happen, and who is responsible when they happen to a horse on trial? If you really want to trial a horse and the seller is willing, make sure the terms of the agreement are clearly set out in writing. They should include details of who is responsible for what costs in the event of the horse's injury, illness or death.

When you are certain that you have found the right horse, you will need to give the seller a deposit (generally 10%). It is essential to set out *in writing* what the buyer and seller are agreeing. For example, it is common for a buyer to agree to purchase subject to the horse being deemed 'suitable for intended use' by a vet (discussed below). Include this in the agreement, with the condition that if the horse is unsuitable your money will be refunded. The agreement should also state what will happen to the deposit if you simply change your mind. You can buy professionally written horse sale and purchase contracts at your local saddlery. These just need to be filled out, and are very helpful in making sure that everyone knows the conditions.

It is important not to be bullied into buying a horse on the spot, unless you are 100% certain. Do not be intimidated by the seller or claims of 'I have other people who want the horse'. The seller may agree to hold the horse for a set period within which you make your decision. If they won't hold it, and the horse gets sold, so be it. There are plenty of other horses and if you weren't 100% sure at the time, it probably wasn't the horse for you.

Be patient. You will probably look at lots of horses before you find the right one.

Vet inspections

It is vital to get the horse inspected by a vet prior to purchase. It is a common misconception in the horse world that a horse will 'pass' or 'fail' the vet check. Claims of horses being '100% sound' in advertisements are misleading as very few horses are 100% sound, just as few people are 100% sound.

Like humans, a horse's physical condition deteriorates as it ages. A person of 40 is probably not as flexible as when they were 15, or they may have a bit of arthritis in an elbow. These problems may not affect their general lifestyle, but if the person was a ballet dancer or a professional tennis player, for example, small problems may prevent them from performing at their peak.

The vet check is to determine whether the horse is sound enough to do what you want it to do. It is essential to tell the vet what you intend to do with the horse. If you are considering an 18-year-old pony for a five-year-old child, the vet will do a basic health check to make sure the horse's heart, lungs, eyes, feet and teeth etc.

are all in good order. The vet would watch the horse walk and trot on a lead or lunge, and inspect its legs for obvious signs of lameness or injury.

If you are considering a six-year-old horse for $50 000, to compete in advanced-level eventing, the vet will do a more extensive inspection, which may include X-rays and an endoscopic examination of the airways.

After inspecting the horse, the vet will discuss their findings and give their opinion on whether the horse is suitable. A little arthritis in the 18-year-old pony's fetlock would probably be acceptable, but the same problem in the six-year-old eventer would be a real concern. It is not always simple to state whether a horse is suitable – the vet may identify a potential future problem but they can't be certain. Under these circumstances the vet will probably indicate the likelihood of the problem progressing, but ultimately it is your decision whether to purchase the horse. Having the horse inspected by a good vet lets you make an informed decision.

> **TIP:** If the vet inspection does identify potential problems you may be able to negotiate a better price. You may be willing to risk a potential problem if you get the horse for a very good price.

Horse accommodation

Fences

If your horse will spend some or all of its time in the paddock it is essential to have good fences. The most common injury sustained by horses involves a leg and a fence. Horses injure their legs by getting them stuck in wire fences; sometimes the injuries are so severe that the horse has to be put down. Horses get stuck as a result of playing or grazing too near a fence, often to be close to a mate on the other side.

There are a number of ways to reduce the risk of your horse getting caught and injured in a fence.

Choosing the right materials

Different types of fences suit different types of animals, for example good-quality sheep fencing is entirely unsuitable for horses. The best types of horse fencing are post-and-rail, synthetic post-and-rail or equine mesh fences. These fences reduce the risk of injury as their materials are very safe. If a horse gets excited and kicks its leg through a timber post-and-rail fence it may get a scratch but the timber is unlikely to cut the horse. This type of fence is also the most expensive.

More common materials in horse fencing are a combination of plain or sight wire and electric wires. Sight wires come in many variations, but generally include white plastic that makes the wire more visible. Plain wire is suitable for horse fencing and can be electrified. Having fewer strands of wire, high off the ground, is better for horses than many strands of wire right down to ground level. This is great fencing for horses but little use for sheep as they will walk straight under it.

Barbed wire is totally unsuitable for horses and should not be used. The same applies to ringlock wire, a mesh wire which is the fencing of choice for sheep. The holes in ringlock are large enough that a horse can put its hoof through the hole. If you use mesh fencing, the holes in the mesh must be smaller than a hoof so that hoofs can't get stuck through the fence.

Keeping horses away from the fence

In a perfect world all horse paddocks would be double-fenced with a gap of roughly 3–4 m between the two fences where two paddocks meet. Trees are often planted in this gap. A gap between adjacent paddocks reduces the incidence of horses playing over the fences and therefore reduces the risk of injury.

Electric fences are also a useful, if not essential, tool for keeping horses away from fences. Electric fences discourage horses from playing and leaning across fences. This not only reduces the risk of injury to your horse but also makes the fence last a lot longer.

Good management of horses also plays a part in reducing the risk of fence injuries. Don't put your horse into a paddock if it or another horse in the area is overly excited. This is especially true when you bring a horse home for the first time – don't put your new horse into the paddock until all its neighbours are happily munching their dinner. If your horse is very excited, lunge it to tire it out or leave it in a yard until it has settled down before putting it in the paddock.

Confined areas

It is essential to have somewhere to confine your horse. A stable is ideal but a yard will do. Sometime, your horse will have an injury that requires confinement. You don't want to have to find a suitable place in the middle of the night after the vet has visited; have something ready just in case.

Stables must be at least 3 m by 3 m, preferably bigger, and lined with timber or bricks. Iron sheeting must be lined as a horse can easily kick through metal. If you plan to build a stable or yard yourself, visit equestrian centres to see well-constructed stables and borrow some good ideas. It is vital to understand the pressure that your construction must withstand. Never skimp on strength – a 500 kg horse can destroy a flimsy stable or injure itself by kicking or rubbing against inferior materials.

TIP: If you are agisting your horse and good stables or yards are not available, you can buy an excellent portable steel yard. These yards are free-standing with interlocking brackets and can be moved as required. Some are quite lightweight and are designed to be carried on the side of your float for use at competitions. They are a good investment.

Riding arenas

Riding arenas, once a rarity, are becoming the norm at club grounds and on private properties. If you intend to school your horse for equestrian competition your task will be much easier with an arena. Riding in your paddock is fine when the weather is good but when the ground is very muddy or hard your horse will struggle. Over the long term, serious riding on hard ground will increase the likelihood of your horse injuring its legs.

With riding arenas you get what you pay for – people who brag about getting their arena built cheaply are recounting disaster stories two years later. All good riding arenas consist of a *very* hard level base with a softer riding surface on top such as sand, rubber or woodchips. A common mistake is to skimp on the base. Some people ignore the base altogether and simply put a riding surface directly onto the ground. This doesn't work. An arena must be built in much the same way as a road. The base should be at least 15 cm thick when compacted, and rolled until it is rock-hard. If you cut into a hill to get a level surface you must include adequate drainage around the arena.

The base must be able to endure the pressure of 500 kg on an area roughly the size of an open hand. This happens when a horse is cantering – when a hind leg first hits the ground and the other three legs are still in the air, the horse's entire weight is resting on one hoof. Over time, a poorly prepared base will deteriorate under this onslaught. Just as a road develops potholes, so will your arena. Holes and soft patches appear, especially around the outside track (outer edge of the riding surface).

The top riding surface needs to be soft but not too deep. Don't make the mistake of having too much riding surface – a surface which is too deep is almost as bad for your horse as riding on rock-hard ground. Approximately 5–10 cm of riding surface is fine. If you need more you can top it up. It is easier and more cost-effective to add more surface than to take a bit away.

You must maintain the arena, as without maintenance this very expensive investment will soon need repair. Furrows will appear along common paths such as the outside track and both sides of jumps. Rake the furrows and move the jumps often to prevent damage to the base. The arena should be harrowed on a regular basis using a metal gate, light harrows or similar towed behind a vehicle.

Floats

If you intend to compete beyond your local area you will need access to a float. Buying a float is a very big investment and you may choose to hire one instead.

Types of floats

Floats come in two basic forms:

- forward-facing (straight load)
- angle-load.

Rear view of an angle-load float.

Traditionally, floats were built using the forward-facing configuration where horses enter the float up a rear ramp and face the front towards the towing vehicle. Now, angle-load floats have become popular. In an angle-load float horses enter via a rear ramp but stand across the float on a 45° angle with their head towards the side/front of the float. Many riders believe that horses travel better on an angle as they can more easily spread their legs apart to remain stable through corners and braking.

Most floats are designed to carry two or three horses; one- and four-horse variations are less common. Single-horse floats are generally only suitable for ponies as their narrow wheelbase reduces their stability, which can be a problem if a large horse gets upset in the float. Even if you only intend to carry one horse, the benefits of purchasing a two-horse float outweigh the additional cost. Not only is it generally easier to load a horse onto a two-horse float, but the additional space is a very handy dressing/dining/sitting room at competitions, especially in the rain.

Choosing a float

Don't be dazzled by fancy paint when choosing a float – it is what's on the inside that counts. Floats need to be very strong, as an upset 500 kg horse can wreck a poorly built float. Check the floor first; the only way to do this is by lying on your back underneath it. Give the floor a good whack with a hammer from underneath (maybe not when the owner is looking!) and make sure it is solid. Float floors rot and must be checked regularly.

A separate front cupboard, usually designed to be accessed from outside, is very handy. Ventilation is also very important. A fully enclosed float must have vents in the roof or walls to allow a good flow of air. Check for rust and whether the axles, brakes, tyres and coupling are up to scratch.

Check the internal horse dividers. It's not important whether the walls or dividers are padded. What counts is whether they're solid. Lock them into place and give them a good shake to see how much they move around; the less movement the better. A straight-loading float has chains or solid rails (breaching gates) which close behind the horse when it is loaded. If possible, choose a float with breaching gates, especially if you intend to carry two horses. The breaching gate locks the first horse into position while you load the second horse, which avoids the common problem of the first horse in the float walking out while you load the second horse. A chain behind the horse does not provide a solid barrier and some horses will panic, run backwards and break the chain.

Check how the dividers, breaching doors and ramp lock into place. They must be easy to do up and undo yet still be very strong. It is also an advantage if dividers, chest bars and breaching doors can be dismantled in an emergency. It's not common, but most experienced horse people can tell of a horse that became entangled in a float and the difficulties of trying to free it.

There are a number of braking systems. Override brakes are essentially emergency brakes which are activated by sudden braking of the tow vehicle – the weight of the trailer closes a gap in the coupling which thus engages the brakes on the trailer. Override brakes are inactive during normal towing, as the towing vehicle's brakes do the vast majority of the float braking. Electric brakes require a special braking unit wired into both the towing vehicle and the float. Electric brakes assist in braking the float during normal use. When the driver brakes in the towing vehicle, the same braking pressure is applied to the float so braking is smooth and safe, especially with heavy floats. If you purchase a float with electric brakes an auto-electrician must fit an electric braking unit to your tow vehicle.

The third braking system, known as 'break-away brakes', occurs on some floats with electric braking systems. This system is designed to bring the float to a halt if it becomes detached from the tow vehicle. A wire is attached to a pin on the float and to the tow vehicle; if the tow vehicle and float are separated the pin is pulled out and the float brakes lock on.

TIP: Floats hold their value well, depending on condition. A float which is kept out of the weather will deteriorate far less than one exposed to the elements. Consider where you intend to keep your float and factor in the cost of building a shed or purchasing a cover for it. The additional cost will be more than recouped by the retained value if you want to resell the float.

Loading

No equestrian activity causes more grief to an inexperienced rider than trying to load a horse onto a float. Tears, tantrums and despair are common emotions in novice horse handlers trying to load a cantankerous horse. The number one rule to remember when loading is that you *cannot* physically manhandle a horse into a float. Even an average-size pony is much stronger than you. No amount of pulling and pushing is going to get the horse onto the float if it doesn't want to go. You must convince the horse that its life will be more comfortable inside the float than outside it.

A professional horse trainer or breaker must train a horse to travel on a float. Putting a horse on a float for the first time is not a job for amateurs. If your horse has had experience travelling on a float and is just trying to make your life difficult, there are a few tricks that should convince it to behave better.

A stubborn little pony may only require a bucket of food in the float and two helpers linking hands behind its rump to encourage it to climb aboard, but this will not be enough for most horses.

Your horse must be trained to come when you pull the reins towards yourself, away from the float. This should be practised daily so it is well established before you try to load the horse. Stand in front of the horse and pull on the reins. If it doesn't move straight away, tap continuously with a whip on the side of its belly until it takes a step forward. Tap hard enough that it is uncomfortable to the horse, but not painful. Good timing is *imperative*. The *instant* the horse takes a step forward you must release the pressure on the reins and stop tapping. If it doesn't step forward continue to tap, if it goes backwards keep tapping. In time the horse will learn that the tapping and rein pressure will continue until it steps forward. Once this training is established away from the float, put your hard work to the test.

The first job is to put the float in the right position. Reduce the avenues of escape by creating visual barriers on either side of the ramp. This can be done by positioning the float in a gateway or yard entrance and closing the gate against one side of the ramp, or by parking the float against the side of a shed. The float must be attached to the tow vehicle during loading, even during a practice load. A free-standing float is not stable and may frighten the horse. Gather some helpers. Two people will be needed to load a difficult horse, but in time and with practice you should be able to load the horse on your own.

When loading a difficult horse in a forward-facing float it is useful to push the centre divider across. This gives the horse a bigger space to move into, but it may be slower to lock the breaching door or chain into place as you probably need to move the divider back first.

Lead the horse towards the float. *Don't* let it turn away from the float. It can go backwards, sideways or dance on the spot, but it must not be allowed to turn around. Horses that are difficult to load often step around to the side of the ramp. It's not necessary to turn the horse around to line it up straight again – even the smallest pony can step up on the side of a ramp. Many western-style floats don't have a ramp at all, and horses simply step up from the ground into the float.

If your horse is difficult to load, put its bridle over the headstall (unclip your lead rope) and hold the reins. Take off the rug and get a long whip (a lunging whip or long dressage whip is fine). Keep it facing the float with pressure on the reins and tap, tap, tap. As soon as the horse takes even half a step forward, release the rein pressure and stop tapping. Give it a pat and pull on the reins again. If it doesn't come forward, start tapping again. Continue this process until the horse is right in the float. Don't hurry, let it move in one step at a time. If you are leading the horse into the float, duck under the chest bar (in a straight-load float) or divider (in an angle-load float) as you load your horse. *Never* get between the horse and the chest bar or be locked in between dividers. The horse can jump forward and crush you in the blink of an eye.

Your helper must be ready to lock the horse into place as soon as it has walked on. This can be a dangerous job and is certainly not for children. On an angle-load float, swing the divider across and lock it into place near the horse's rump. Stand near the end of the divider – if the horse panics and runs backwards out of the float you don't want to be trapped between the open divider and the wall. On a straight-load float make sure you are never directly behind the horse. Depending on the type of door or chain, reach across from the side or centre of the ramp. It is important to avoid standing where a horse can send a half-closed breaching door swinging into your face. If there are chains to secure the horse into position in a straight-load float, it might be easier to close the ramp and lock it in place as soon as the horse is loaded. This is best done with a person on either side of the ramp. Once the ramp is up you can travel the horse with the divider swung across (which many horses prefer), or reach over the ramp to slide the divider into position and secure the chain.

When the horse is securely in position with the ramp closed, clip your lead rope back onto the headstall and take off the bridle. Always tie up your horse in the float. Horses can turn around in a very small area and many people have stories about arriving at their destination to find their horse's head peering over the top of the ramp at them.

Horses that are very difficult to load into the float require professional help. A good breaker or trainer can teach your horse and give you practical training in loading techniques.

> **TIP:** If you are travelling a single horse in a double straight-loading float, always put it on the right-hand (driver's) side. The camber of the road makes the float tip slightly to the left, so by putting the horse on the right you are balancing the float. If you have two horses, always put the heavier horse on the right-hand side.

Unloading

Before starting to unload, make sure you are in a safe environment. It is easy to lose control of a horse when unloading, so it is important to be in a confined area such as a fenced area with the gate shut. If the venue is not fenced, unload away from roads but remain close to other horses. If you do lose control of the horse, it is less likely to run away if there are other horses about.

Unloading one horse from a float is relatively straightforward, but more thought is required when you have two or more horses. For a single horse in a straight-load float, first untie the horse. If you are on your own hang the end of the lead rope over the horse's neck; if you have a helper they should stand in the front of the float with the horse. If there are chains behind your horse and it tends to rush out of the float, undo the chain before you open the ramp. In floats with breaching doors, the horse will remain secure with the ramp down and the breaching doors closed. Never remove the rear barriers without untying the horse first!

> **TIP:** Never stand directly behind a ramp that you are opening or closing. Always stand to the side, especially if you are using a float with chains. You will be crushed by the ramp if a horse rushes out while you are standing directly behind it. Always be careful of children. Ensure they are well clear before you open or close a ramp.

If you have a helper, ask them to open the rear barrier. Gently encourage your horse to back out of the float *slowly*, duck under the chest bar and follow it out. Be prepared for the horse to panic and run backwards. Make sure the lead rope is not wrapped around your hand. If the horse moves too fast just let it go – you are not strong enough to hold a panicking horse and will just end up with rope burn. When unloading on your own, stand to the side of the ramp and click your tongue to encourage your horse to walk out. As its neck gets to the back of the float, grab the lead rope which is hanging across its neck.

Unloading two horses from a straight-load float is best done with two people. The challenge is the musketeer effect, 'All for one and one for all'. When the first horse is unloaded the second horse generally wants to join it immediately. If there are chains behind the horses, untie both horses and both chains at the same time. A horse left in the float with just a chain can rush out and break the chain or, worse still, push on the chain and pull the divider in against itself. This causes even greater panic.

One person stands in the front of the float and holds both horses. They put the lead rope over the neck of the first horse and hold the horse that will remain in the float. Encourage the first horse to come out and have the helper outside the float grab the rope as the horse backs out. The helper inside the float can then walk out

Forward-facing float with very good breaching gates.

with the second horse. If the second horse isn't keen on waiting in the float it doesn't matter – the horses can walk off safely together as long as there is one person in control of each horse.

> **TIP:** If your float has chains a float builder can easily replace them with breaching gates.

Angle-load floats are very handy when you have to load and unload multiple horses alone, as a horse is secure once it is locked behind an angle barrier. Unloading horses from an angle-load float is really a one-person job. As with a straight-load float, untie the horse before you open the divider. Pass the lead rope over the horse's neck and move to the end of the divider at the horse's rump. Make sure the horse isn't leaning against the divider, then open it and walk between the divider and the horse to its head, and take hold of the lead rope. It is not uncommon for a horse to walk off the float at an angle and therefore risk falling off the edge of the ramp. If the horse is coming off at the wrong angle you can straighten it up by pulling its head in the opposite direction to which you want its rump to go, like reversing in a car. If the rump is too far to the right (which is usually the case), pull the head over to the right and the rump generally moves to the left.

Repeat this for each horse in the angle-load float. Don't have one person standing with the horse between closed dividers while another opens the dividers. If the horse panics the result could be fatal.

> **TIP:** Smaller horses and ponies may turn around in an angle-load float while being unloaded, and walk out of the float forwards. This is fine. Be ready – stand right up near its head. If you are standing at the shoulder and the horse marches out forwards you might end up with a squashed toe.

Driving with the float

Do a quick safety inspection before *every single trip*. First and foremost make sure that the float is correctly attached to the towing vehicle. Check and recheck that the coupling is locked down. Leaving the coupling unlocked is an easy mistake to make, as most modern couplings can be locked open so that you don't have to hold them while winding down the jockey wheel. If you leave the coupling unlocked, you may find the float sitting with the coupling in the mud while you try to load. The worst-case scenario does not bear thinking about – security chains are useless if they are the only thing holding a fully loaded float being towed at speed.

> **TIP:** Do you know the towing laws for your state? Do you know the towing capacity of your vehicle? What is the towing capacity of your towbar? What size towball do you have? What size towball does your coupling require? Do you know the weight of your loaded float? Do some research before you hit the road. Failure to meet specifications could end in disaster.

Check that all your lights are working and that your break-away breaks and safety chains are attached. Ensure your tyres, including the spare, are in good condition and well-inflated. Make sure that your spare tyre, and the tools required to change it, are with you. If you get a flat tyre on your float it is best not to jack up the float as restless horses may cause the jack to dislodge. As floats have two tyres on each side, it is better to drive the good tyre on the problem side up onto a small platform (available through float suppliers). This will leave the flat tyre on that side suspended above the ground for you to change.

Towing a horse float can be very dangerous for you and the horse, as you are dealing with a very heavy and moving weight. The number one rule of towing is to do it *slowly*. Imagine standing in a bus with no rail to hold. How fast could the bus brake, accelerate or turn a corner before you lost your balance? This is what the horse must do, and although its four legs give a balance advantage over your two, it must still work quite hard to maintain its footing. Slow right down to take a corner, <15 km/h is appropriate for a right-angle turn. Slow even more if you hear or feel the horse moving in the float.

Acceleration should be *slow and even*. Avoid jerky starts. Watch your speed – travelling at the speed limit is often too fast as you cannot safely brake as hard as normal. Travelling at 100 km/h with a horse float is rarely safe. A poorly balanced float can be sent into a fishtail skid by even a small bump in the road if it hits at high speed. The weight of a fishtailing float can tip both car and float over.

Even if you have electric brakes on the float, you must dramatically adjust your braking technique when towing a float. You may be able to stop the vehicles in a reasonably short distance with electric brakes, but you may find your horse in the back seat of your car! You must brake very slowly, or risk the horse falling over in the float. You need far more distance to brake safely with a float than you normally require, so leave sufficient space between you and the vehicle in front.

> **TIP:** Horses spread their legs apart to maintain their balance, just as we do when standing on a train or bus. Don't have dividers that are solid all the way to the floor – the horse will be much happier if it can spread its legs slightly under the divider.

Saddles

Types of saddles

There are four basic styles of English saddle used in the equestrian sports discussed in this book:

- dressage
- turnout
- jumping
- all-purpose.

Each type is designed to optimise the rider's position in the chosen discipline. In very simple terms, a rider on the flat (dressage or hacking) has a longer stirrup length than a rider who is jumping. The shorter the rider's stirrups, the tighter the angle of the rider's knee. As the stirrup shortens and the knee angle tightens, the rider's knee naturally moves forward to maintain the desired balance position. A straight vertical line through the rider's ear, shoulder, hip and heel is the ideal balance position in any discipline.

To compete in the dressage or show arenas you need a dressage or turnout saddle. For jumping, an all-purpose saddle is acceptable at lower levels but you will need a specialised jumping saddle as you move up the ranks. To a newcomer who is dabbling in all disciplines or taking on eventing, the all-purpose saddle seems the logical choice for both the flat and the jumps. This is not the case. An all-purpose saddle is usually unsuitable for either the flat or jumps – it is too forward-cut for riding on the flat and too deep-seated for riding the jumps. Most riders struggle to maintain the correct position in an all-purpose saddle as it is designed to be halfway between the correct dressage and correct jumping position – and that is the position you usually slip into when using one.

If funds are limited but you want to ride on the flat and over the jumps, buy two cheaper (second-hand) well-fitting saddles, one for jumping and one for riding on the flat, instead of an expensive all-purpose saddle.

Dressage saddles
Dressage saddles are used by most competitors in the dressage arena but are also used in the show ring. Most professional show riders use their turnout saddle only for turnout classes and use a dressage saddle for all other events. Viewed side on, the front flap of a dressage saddle runs in roughly a vertical line, from the pommel to the bottom of the saddle flap. The front flap may be curved slightly forward, the degree of curvature varying from brand to brand. Dressage saddles are generally higher at the cantle and have a deeper seat than a jumping saddle. A dressage saddle slopes gently down from the pommel then rises more steeply to the top of the cantle. The cantle is always higher, in some cases quite a bit higher, than the pommel; the higher the cantle the deeper the seat.

Dressage saddles usually have long girth points, which means that the girth does up below the bottom of the saddle flap and the girth buckles are visible. Some dressage saddles have short points where the girth does up under the saddle flap. Most dressage riders prefer long girth points as they reduce bulk under the saddle flap and allow their legs to rest more easily against the horse's side.

Dressage saddles are available in various shades of brown from light tan to deep mahogany or black. Black has traditionally been the colour of choice in the dressage arena and brown is generally used in the show ring, although this is really a matter of preference. In the show ring it is not uncommon for riders to select a saddle colour that coordinates well with their horse's coat. Brown saddles are used on chestnuts, bay and brown horses, while blacks and greys may look better in black.

> **TIP:** If you are planning to use your dressage saddle in the show ring stick to the more classically styled dressage saddles. Avoid saddles with suede inserts or overly large knee rolls, as they are not elegant enough for the show ring.

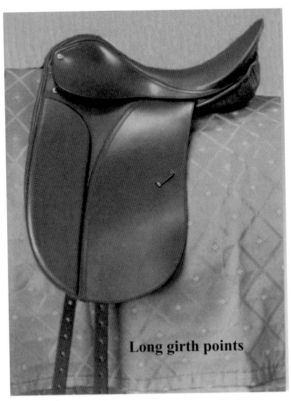

Long girth points

Dressage saddle with long girth points. Photo: Malcolm Byrne Saddlery

Turnout saddles

Turnout saddles are similar to dressage saddles, with two key differences. A turnout saddle has covered buttons on either side of the saddle just below the pommel, covered with leather to match the saddle. On a dressage saddle these buttons are metallic and often bear the name of the saddle manufacturer.

The second distinctive feature of a turnout saddle is the girth points. A turnout saddle must have three short girth points with a matching three-buckle leather girth, to be entirely correct.

Jumping saddles

The knee flap of a jumping saddle is quite forward-cut. When viewed from the side it has a distinct curve towards the front of the horse. The seat of a jumping saddle is quite flat with a very slight downward slope from the pommel and a gentle rise to the cantle, which is only slightly higher than the pommel. The forward-cut knee flap, combined with the flat seat, allow the rider to maintain their balance position by sliding to the back of the saddle and reducing their knee angle as required.

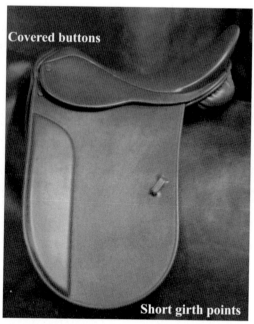

Turnout saddle. Photo: Malcolm Byrne Saddlery

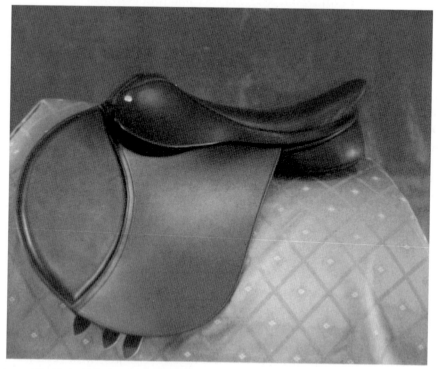

Jumping saddle. Photo: Malcolm Byrne Saddlery

All-purpose saddles

A hybrid between dressage and jumping saddles, an all-purpose saddle is only suitable for low-level jumping or pleasure riding. Trying to ride competitively in an all-purpose saddle is difficult, and often very frustrating for an inexperienced competition rider.

Saddle fit

Saddle fit: the horse

Fit is the number one criterion for choosing a saddle. A poorly fitting saddle is not only painful for your horse but makes the task of riding much harder, as it works against your vertical ear/shoulder/hip/heel line. Having your saddle professionally fitted is worthwhile, and most good saddlery stores offer this service. Although there are many saddle-fitting problems, two of the most common are a forward-tipping saddle and a backward-tipping saddle.

If a saddle tips too far forward it may rest on the horse's wither and cause pain. There should always be a gap of roughly 5 cm between the horse's wither and the pommel when you are sitting on the saddle. Even if the saddle has sufficient clearance on the wither, it may still tip you forward if the lowest point of the saddle (viewed side-on) is too near the front of the saddle. If the lowest point of the seat is just behind the pommel, your leg will be forced too far back and your body will tip forward.

The more common problem is a saddle that tips too far back. When viewed side-on, the lowest point of the seat is towards the back of the saddle. This saddle fit pushes you into a 'chair' seat position with your lower leg too far forward and your bottom towards the back of the saddle, like you sit in a chair.

A poorly fitting saddle makes the difficult task of equestrian competition riding even harder. Have your saddle professionally fitted before you buy it. Although some saddles can be adjusted, the saddle you want to buy just might not fit your horse. It's best to find out before you hand over the cash.

> **TIP:** Some saddles have interchangeable or adjustable gullets, a part of the internal frame which determines saddle width. These saddles can be a good choice as they fit a large number of horse types. You may not need to buy a new saddle just because you buy a new horse.

Saddle fit: the rider

Saddles come in different sizes to fit different riders, starting at roughly 14 inches (31 cm) for small children up to 18 inches (40 cm) for large adults. The size of a saddle is measured from the button on the side of the saddle near the pommel, to the top of the cantle at the back. Saddles are usually sized in ½ inch (1 cm) increments, with 16–17 inch (36–38 cm) saddles the most common. Although the size of the saddle is only a measurement of the seat, the saddle flap increases in proportion. That is, the saddle flap on a 15 inch (33 cm) saddle is shorter than the saddle flap on a 17 inch (38 cm) saddle.

Get the right size saddle, and don't let vanity rule your decision! Don't try to squeeze a 17½ inch backside into a 15½ inch saddle because you think the larger saddle looks too chunky. You can't ride effectively if you are jammed into position. Conversely, you don't want a saddle so big you could invite a friend along. The saddlery store will help you determine the correct size – follow that advice.

Bridles

Bridles fall into two basic categories – snaffle bridles and double or Weymouth bridles. A snaffle bridle is used with a single bit, while a double bridle is used with two bits. Some riders purchase a double bridle and remove the additional bit strap when they want to use it as a snaffle bridle.

> **TIP:** It is easy to get your bridle into a muddle when changing it between a double and snaffle bridle. On a double bridle, the snaffle bit (bridoon) always attaches to the loose removable strap, while a Weymouth/curb bit attaches to the fixed headpiece. The removable bridoon strap buckle should always be on the horse's right-hand side.

Most differences between bridles are primarily cosmetic, but there are two areas where bridle design has a significant impact on function – the noseband and the reins.

Nosebands

The noseband is not for decoration. It discourages the horse from opening its mouth too wide. If a horse works with its mouth open the bit will not work effectively. A noseband should be firm but not tight; you should be able to comfortably slide two fingers side-by-side between the noseband and the horse's face.

There are four basic noseband types and a multitude of variations within each type.

Cavesson noseband

A cavesson noseband is a single loop of leather that sits above the bit and 3–4 cm below the horse's cheekbone. This is a very simple noseband and the least effective at closing a horse's mouth, as it sits above the bit. The cavesson is the only noseband type that can be used with a double bridle when riding on the flat. The cavesson is the noseband of choice in the show ring as it is the most flattering to the horse's head.

Double dressage bridle. All double bridles are worn with cavesson nosebands. Photo: Malcolm Byrne Saddlery

Hanoverian noseband

A Hanoverian noseband (also known as a flash noseband) is a cavesson noseband with an additional strap through a loop on the front of the cavesson. The additional strap is secured around the horse's mouth immediately below the bit. The Hanoverian is more effective in closing the horse's mouth as it sits below the bit. Hanoverian nosebands are very popular with snaffle bridles for dressage and jumping.

Cavesson and Hanoverian nosebands are both suitable options for someone starting out.

> **TIP:** By removing the leather strap on a Hanoverian noseband you can turn it into a cavesson, except this leaves an unattractive loop on the front of the noseband. To overcome this, some bridles are made with removable Hanoverian loops. These let you remove the loop altogether, leaving a plain cavesson. Purchasing a bridle that has a Hanoverian noseband with removable loop gives the flexibility of having both a cavesson and Hanoverian noseband.

Jumping bridle with Hanoverian noseband and reins with a loop attachment. Photo: Malcolm Byrne Saddlery

Crossover noseband

Crossover nosebands are made of two long straps which thread through a leather or sheepskin disc to form a cross. One strap passes high around the nose near and sometimes above the cheekbone; the second strap passes around the horse's mouth immediately below the bit. These nosebands provide a pressure point on the horse's nose, as well as directly affecting the mouth and jaw to discourage the horse from opening its mouth. Riders often use these nosebands for jumping, and to a lesser extent in the dressage arena.

Drop noseband

Once very popular, this type of noseband is now much less common. Most riders use a Hanoverian to achieve much the same outcome. A drop noseband has a single strap that passes around the mouth immediately below the bit. It works entirely on the horse's mouth without any pressure on the upper jaw.

Show bridles

Show bridles can be flat or raised. Showing nosebands are unadorned but browbands are another matter altogether! Coloured ribbon browbands are all the rage, often with diamanté rosettes on each side. Younger riders often wear a lapel rosette and hairclips in their plaits which match the horse's browband. Decorations are not appropriate in turnout and hunter horse classes.

Show bridles are made with narrower pieces of leather and are generally finer than their dressage equivalent. A perfectly fitting turnout bridle should have each buckle in the fourth hole, with the buckles forming a horizontal line. The only way to achieve this is to have the bridle made to measure your horse, but this is expensive. Don't compromise on the fit of your horse's bridle by having buckles too tight or too loose, just to line up the buckles!

Dressage bridles

Dressage riders generally steer away from coloured browbands (except in pony/riding club) and decorate their bridles with contrasting leather backing on the noseband and browband, which gives the appearance of coloured piping. Backing is usually white or cream, but more adventurous colours are popping up. Gold or silver chains teamed with matching rosettes/shields are also popular adornments for dressage browbands.

Dressage bridles are made with wider leather than showing bridles, and it is not unusual to see a dressage noseband which is twice as wide as a show noseband. These heavier-looking bridles suit the heavier and more masculine heads common in warmbloods. When choosing a dressage bridle, have a good look at your horse's head size and shape before you think about a chunky and highly adorned model. If your horse has a fine thoroughbred head it may look overwhelmed by a big dressage bridle – try teaming a chain browband with a finer show bridle. This can be a good choice for fine thoroughbreds competing in eventing dressage.

Jumping bridles

You don't need a separate bridle for the cross-country and showjumping phases of a horse trials event, but you probably need a separate set of reins for the jumping phase.

Form rather than fashion is important for jumping bridles, especially for cross-country. Make sure the leather is a reasonable thickness, soft and supple and in good condition. Don't use very fine show bridles for cross-country jumping, as the narrow leather can stretch and weaken under extreme conditions.

Reins

Reins for equestrian competition are generally made from leather, rubber or plastic, or combinations of these. Leather reins may be smooth and plain, or the grip may be enhanced by leather cleats at regular intervals along the reins. Leather lacing is also used to enhance the grip on leather reins, the raised lacing providing a more secure hand position.

Rubber and plastic reins provide superior grip, especially in the rain, and are often favoured by cross-country riders. They are also stronger than leather reins and are less likely to break.

There are three common methods of attaching the reins to the bit – traditional buckles, metal hooks known as billets, or fixed loops. Traditional buckles provide a secure attachment to the bit and can be used on the flat or when jumping but are less popular in the show ring as they can look a little chunky on a fine show bridle.

Billets are small hooks which pass through a hole in the attaching piece of leather to give a neat look without the bulk of a full buckle. Billets are used on most bridles to secure the cheekstrap to the bit/s. These attachments are safe to use on reins when riding on the flat but should *never* be used when jumping. Under extreme pressure the billet can pull through the leather, detaching the rein. Some associations do not allow this type of rein attachment when jumping – check the rule book.

The third method of attaching reins is to use a loop sewn into the end of each rein. The rein is attached by threading its end through the loop and pulling it tight against the bit. This type of rein attachment is very safe and the best choice when riding cross-country.

Bits and pieces

The choice of bits is truly staggering – just have a look in any saddlery and you will be overwhelmed! Bits have two basic parts. There is a mouthpiece which sits in the horse's mouth, and the rings or cheeks which sit outside the mouth and onto which the reins and bridle are attached. Work closely with your instructor to find the bit that best suits your horse.

There are four general categories of bits in equestrian sports: snaffles, Weymouth/curbs, gags and hackamores.

Snaffles

Snaffles are the simplest type and a good place to start. Snaffle mouthpieces may be unjointed or have one or two joins in the middle. They are usually made of metal but can be made of rubber or rubber-coated metal. A double-jointed snaffle with a rounded centrepiece (lozenge) is a good choice, as it is a gentle bit which most horses find comfortable.

A bridoon is a snaffle bit with a thinner mouthpiece and a smaller ring to allow it to sit better when used with a Weymouth as part of a 'bit and bridoon' or double bridle.

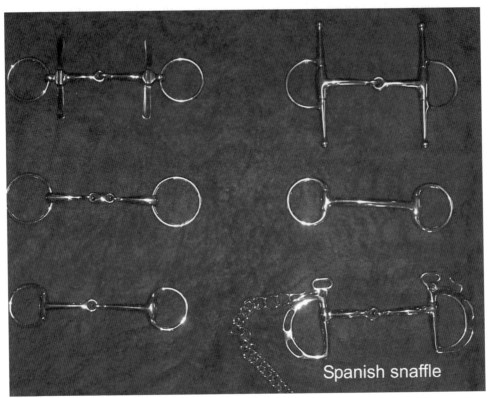

Spanish snaffle

A small selection of snaffle bits. Spanish snaffles can never be used in competitions where rules specify a snaffle bit must be used, including all dressage competitions. Photo: Melton Saddlery

A Spanish snaffle is *not* a snaffle under dressage rules and cannot be worn in dressage competition. A Spanish snaffle has a chain and lever action as described below, and should be treated with a high level of respect.

TIP: Metallic bits can be nickel-plated, stainless steel or silver compounds. Avoid the nickel-plated bits, as they rust and will cost you more in the long run.

TIP: Read your rule book very carefully when it comes to bits. Make sure your bit complies, or you may be sent home early.

Weymouth/curbs (double bridle)
A Weymouth/curb bit is worn with a bridoon to form a double bridle. A curb bit is *never* used on its own. It takes skill to correctly fit a double bridle so that the two

bits sit comfortably and effectively in the horse's mouth. A double bridle always uses a chain which passes under the horse's chin and attaches to either side of the curb bit. The chain has a leather cover and is attached with a leather lip strap for the show ring, but dressage riders don't always use a cover, and lip straps in the dressage arena are very rare.

Two sets of reins must be used, one set attached to the bridoon and the other thinner set attached to the ring at the end of the lever on the curb bit. This lever and chain make the bit dangerous in inexperienced hands. Like any lever, the pressure that is transferred to the horse's chin via the curb chain is far greater than the actual pressure applied by the rider's hands. A skilful rider can use the two sets of reins independently, applying pressure to either the bridoon or curb bit as required. A less-experienced rider can't apply pressure independently and will inadvertently apply pressure to both bits, sending confusing signals to the horse. This type of bit/bridle is *not* suitable for beginners.

In the dressage arena, double bridles may only be used by competitors in the higher grades (EFA medium and above).

In the show ring, double bridles can be used by competitors of any experience except in specific classes where the program states, for example, 'pleasure pony'. If you are showing, don't be too anxious to start using a double bridle. Your horse must work in the correct outline (on the bit) in a snaffle bit. If you can't get your horse to work well on the bit in a snaffle, pulling its head with a double bridle is not the answer.

> **TIP:** Some riders consider that a Pelham bit is a good compromise between a snaffle and a double bridle. A Pelham has a single mouthpiece with two rings on the cheek. One ring is at the top in the bridoon position and the other is at the bottom in the curb position. The Pelham has a chain in the same position as the double bridle. This bit is unsuitable for inexperienced riders because it is just as severe on the horse as a double bridle – the lever action, not the number of mouthpieces, affects the horse most.

Gags

Gags differ from other bits as they work primarily on the horse's poll rather than the mouth. Most gags work with a lever action but do not use a chain. The lever applies strong pressure on the horse's poll, which can be very effective at stopping a strong horse on a jumping course. Like double bridles, gags should only be used by experienced riders.

Gags are never used in the dressage or show arenas. Whether they are allowed for cross-country or showjumping depends on the association, so check your rule book.

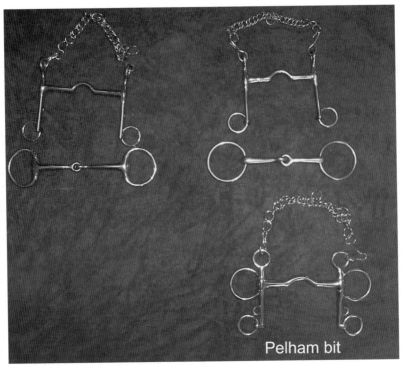

Different Weymouth and bridoon sets. The Pelham bit cannot be used in dressage competitions but is quite popular in the show ring among younger riders. Photo: Melton Saddlery

Hackamores

A hackamore is a bit without a mouthpiece. The hackamore is fitted with a large padded band which sits on the horse's nose and a chain which passes under the horse's chin; no part of the bit goes into the horse's mouth. The long cheeks of the hackamore provide a lever action which applies pressure to the horse's nose, which is very effective at stopping a strong horse. However, the hackamore is not nearly as good for turning a horse! If you ride a jumping course with a hackamore you may find that you have no steering. More advanced riders use a snaffle and hackamore together with two sets of reins. A skilful rider can work two sets of reins independently, using one set to steer and the other to control the speed. Hackamores should only be used by very experienced riders and are never permitted in pony club competitions.

Safety equipment

Helmets are the most important piece of equestrian safety equipment and should be worn at all times. Each association requires helmets to meet a specific Australian or European design standard. These standards are continually

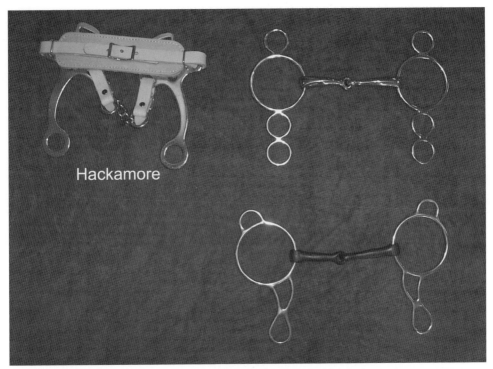

Hackamore

Some styles of gags. The hackamore is a very strong bit which should only be used by very experienced riders. Photo: Melton Saddlery

upgraded, so make sure your helmet meets the required standard before you start competing. Young children must develop the habit of putting on their helmet before handling their horse, to give additional protection if the horse kicks out.

Back protectors are common, particularly among cross-country riders. They are compulsory for EFA cross-country riders and some pony clubs insist that members wear them when jumping. It is not unusual for younger riders to wear them all the time. Most back protectors sold in Australia provide similar levels of safety, but the more expensive lightweight models are more comfortable, especially in summer.

Most riders are terrified of falling off their horse and having a foot stuck in the stirrup. Using the correct size stirrup will reduce the risk of getting your foot stuck, and using toe stops will virtually eliminate it. Toe stops (young children use clogs) attach to the front of the stirrup and curve around your toe, forming a barrier which prevents your foot sliding too far through the stirrup. They are an excellent safety device which are essential for children and worthwhile for all cross-country riders. Check the rule book before using toe stops in dressage events, as rules vary between associations.

Rugs

If you wish to compete you will need to rug your horse. Rugs perform a number of roles – they keep your horse clean, prevent its coat being bleached by the sun, protect it in the cold and wet and provide some relief from summer flies. Rugs are expensive and you get what you pay for. Cheap rugs are usually inferior in material and fit and cost more in the long run as they need more frequent replacement. All rugs have a limited lifespan. Depending on how rough your horse is, you will need to replace everyday rugs every one to three years.

There are four basic rug styles: rugs, neck rugs, hoods and combos. A rug is fastened across the horse's chest in front and secured behind with straps between the horse's hind legs. It may also have straps under the horse's belly for additional security.

A neck rug wraps around the horse's neck from behind its ears to over the top of the rug. It is attached to the rug with clips that prevent it sliding over the horse's head. A neck rug cannot be worn without a rug to attach it to. The downside is that neck rugs tend to slip around and there is always a risk of the rug attachments breaking or coming undone, which can result in the neck rug slipping over the horse's head.

A hood is an extended neck rug covering the horse's neck and face. The hood has holes for the horse's ears and eyes and is fastened under its neck and jaw. Cotton hoods should only be used in the paddock if absolutely necessary, as it is quite easy for a hood to come undone or be torn in such a way that it covers the horse's eyes. Some horses will wait in the paddock with the 'blindfold' in place until you rescue them, but others will panic and run blindly into fences or trees. Canvas hoods are very dangerous as the strong material does not tear easily. They should be used with extreme caution in the paddock or avoided altogether.

Combo rugs are a rug and neck rug joined together permanently. A combo neck rug is less likely to slip around, and as it is virtually impossible for it to slip over the horse's head it is a very safe choice. The shortcoming is that you cannot use the rug on its own and if the horse tears part of the rug you must replace it all. This is a small price to pay for the advantages of better fit and safety.

Three basic rug sets are needed:

- a cotton/summer paddock rug and neck rug or combo
- a cotton competition set rug and hood/neck rug or combo
- a winter/waterproof set rug and neck rug or combo.

You can buy additional rugs as well if finances permit:

- rain sheet
- woollen dress rug (or you could win one at a competition).

Cotton/summer paddock rugs

A horse usually wears this rug all the time, as a full wardrobe in warmer months and as an underrug during winter. There are a number of synthetic summer rugs but cotton is still the best choice as it works well as both a summer rug and an underrug. I am a little sceptical about the comfort of a synthetic summer rug – if I had to stand in the sun I would prefer a cotton shirt to a plastic one, even if the plastic one had air holes.

A paddock rug must be robust, as horses are very tough on rugs. Cotton rugs must be made of heavy-duty cotton with ripstop thread to stop them tearing badly when the horse decides to scratch against a tree. The best colour is white, as that is coolest in the hot sun.

Combo rugs are a great choice as they fit well and are safe.

Cotton competition or dress rugs

These rugs spend most of their time in the cupboard, only being used the night before and on the day of a competition. A competition set should include a rug, a hood or neck rug and a tail bag. If your horse is spending the night before a competition in the paddock, choose a neck rug. If it will be confined in a stable or yard a hood will keep it cleaner. A tail bag slides over the horse's tail and attaches to the underside of the rug, to keep the tail clean.

These rugs do not need to be as robust as paddock rugs and rarely use ripstop thread. They are available in many colour combinations and some competitors match the rug colour to their float colour.

> **TIP:** If a horse will be wearing dress rugs in the paddock the night before a competition, put the paddock rug over the top or the good rugs will end up filthy.

Winter rugs

Winter rugs are made of canvas or a synthetic material. Canvas rugs are heavier than synthetic rugs and lose their waterproof qualities over time. Like cotton paddock rugs, most good canvas rugs have ripstop thread woven into the material; cheaper versions without ripstop thread will not last long in the paddock. Canvas rugs are lined with a wool or synthetic blanket, whose thickness and quality greatly affect the cost.

Synthetic rugs are a good choice for winter as they provide warmth and waterproof qualities without excessive weight. The lighter weight is especially good when the rug is wet and muddy – a wet canvas rug can be very difficult for a child or adult with shoulder problems to lift on and off the horse.

A winter neck rug does not need to be as warm as the rug. It is common to use a canvas neck rug with no lining, or a synthetic neck rug without filling. Neck rugs tend to rub out the horse's mane as it lowers and raises its head to eat, so the lighter the neck rug the less likely it is to rub out the mane.

Neither synthetic nor canvas winter neck rugs stay in place well. Also, the join between the neck rug and the rug allows water to enter when the horse has its head down grazing. A combo is a great choice as winter rug, as long as you check that the neck rug section is lighter than the body part.

Always use a cotton rug under a winter rug. You can keep your horse relatively clean by washing the cotton underrug every few weeks. A winter rug on the horse's skin will get very dirty and end up covered in hair as the horse moults. Dirty winter rugs are virtually impossible to wash.

> **TIP:** Warmer is not always better when it comes to winter rugs. In many parts of Australia winter is not very cold, and the warmest synthetic rugs are too hot. Most synthetic rugs advise a temperature range where the rug will be comfortable, e.g. 8–15°. Discuss your needs with the saddlery and choose a rug suited to the local climate.

Rain sheets

Rain sheets are winter rugs without the warmth. Unlined canvas rugs or synthetic rugs without filling are the most common types of rain sheets. These rugs are great for nighttime in the summer and all day during late autumn and early spring. You can put a rain sheet over the top of dress rugs in the paddock or stable to keep them clean, or at a competition to provide a little extra warmth.

Woollen dress rugs

Woollen dress rugs are used as underrugs to provide additional warmth, or over the top of cotton dress rugs in the stable or at competition. A woollen rug is very handy at competition as it can be thrown over the top of a horse with its saddle still on between events, and is light and clean. If you only have a winter rug at competition it will quickly become covered in mud, which ends up on your clean clothes as you put the rug on and off the horse.

Bibs

As the name suggests, a bib sits around the horse's neck and covers its shoulders. Made of, or lined with, a satin-type material, a bib helps prevent rub marks on the horse's shoulders from the rug. Many rugs have shoulder gussets which open as the horse moves, and greatly reduce the risk of rubbed shoulders.

TIP: Horse rugs are measured in feet and inches, from just under 4 ft for very small ponies to over 7 ft for the biggest horses. Measure from the centre of your horse's chest, where the rug will be buckled around its body, to the side of its rump in line with the top of its tail (dock). Getting the right size is very important – rugs which are too large can slip behind the horse's wither and cause nasty rubs on the back and shoulders. A rug that is too small will be uncomfortable, restricting movement and rubbing the shoulders. Most saddleries let you exchange a rug if you purchase the wrong size, as long as you put clean towels over the horse when trying the rug for size. Saddleries won't exchange if the rug has been worn or is covered in hair.

Feeding

If your horse is too fat or too skinny you must deal with it immediately. Horse nutrition is a very complex subject with entire books devoted to the topic; this section only touches on the subject. However, average competition riders will find that feeding a horse is relatively straightforward unless it is suffering from a specific condition.

Like humans:

Energy in > energy out = horse puts on weight
Energy in < energy out = horse loses weight

As grazing animals, horses need a lot of roughage, most often through grass or hay. Ponies and some horses require only this sort of food when being ridden by a child. Bigger horses doing more work or horses/ponies on poor or dry pasture will need feed supplements.

The easiest and most cost-effective way to feed one or two horses is to use a premixed feed. Most of these feeds are well-balanced and have a number of variations tailored to suit different energy levels. For example, there is a low-energy 'pony club' mix for horses in light work and a high-energy 'racing mix' for horses that work harder. Follow the bag's instructions about how to introduce a new feed into the horse's diet and how much roughage to give in conjunction with the feed. Most feeds have comprehensive feeding guides on their websites and some will even create an individual feeding program.

Horses do not gain or lose weight overnight. It is a slow process and you need to keep a close eye on the horse to catch any unwanted changes in weight before they are too dramatic. If you catch the change early you can adjust the feeding program accordingly.

Signs that a horse is getting too thin:

- ribs can be seen easily
- horse's spine is protruding behind the saddle and over the rump
- grooves on the rump either side of the horse's tail (poverty lines) become obvious
- girth is done up in further holes.

Signs that a horse is getting too fat (a common problem in ponies):

- horse's crest (top of the neck where the mane grows) is hard and thick
- when viewed from behind, the rump is higher on either side than the spine
- ribs cannot be felt when you push into the horse's side
- girth is getting more difficult to do up.

Parasite control is essential in maintaining your horse's weight and its general health. Worm burden is a key cause of colic in horses. Worm your horse regularly and keep paddocks as clean as possible to break the worm lifecycle.

TIP: Don't fall into the trap of giving many different feeds and supplements. It is expensive, time-consuming and unnecessary. Most horses will get all the nutrients they need from good pasture and a reputable premixed feed. If your horse is too thin, just feed it more. If your horse is too fat, feed it less.

Summary

Having the right tools for the job is essential in any pursuit, and equestrian sports are no exception. Equestrian equipment is expensive and you don't need the best of everything on day one to succeed. Good basics are the key. The priorities are a safe horse, a well-fitting saddle and bridle, and quality helmet and boots. Over time you can accumulate additional equipment and upgrade your basics. Don't obsess over the equipment you would like but can't afford – there is nothing to be gained by this. Winning the blue ribbon does not depend on whether you arrive in a solid old float with flaking paint or in a brand-new shiny one.

Appendix 1: Dressage arenas

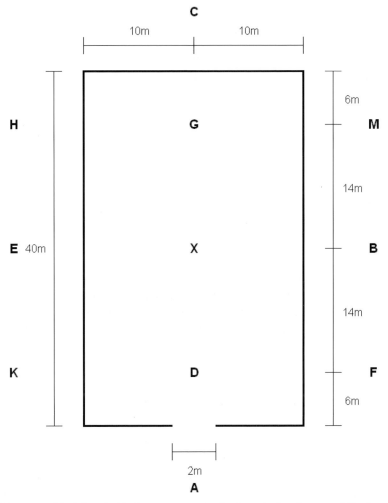

A 40 m × 20 m arena. The letters inside the arena are not actually marked on the ground. You have to judge their positions by using the letters around the outside of the arena. For example, a test may say to 'Halt at X' – you know that X lies between E and B along the A to C line. A good way to remember key letters of the arena is **A F**at **B**lack **M**other **C**at **H**ad **E**ight **K**ittens.

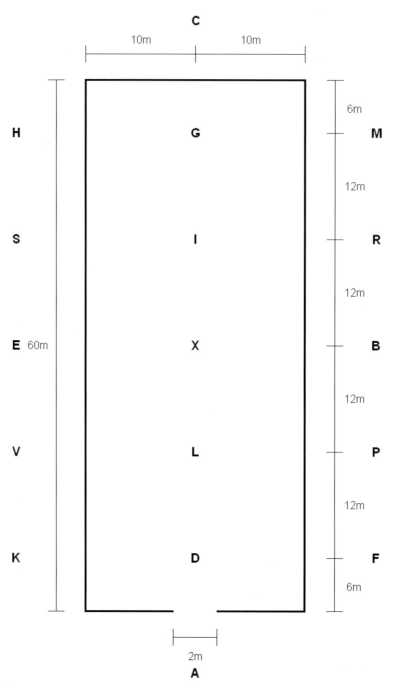

A 60 m × 20 m arena.

Appendix 2: Example dressage test

Level *X*, Test *Y*
Arena 60 m × 20 m or 40 m × 20 m
To be ridden in an ordinary snaffle.
All trot work may be either rising or sitting unless specified.
Number _____ Horse name _____
Rider _____

Test			Max marks	Judge's mark	Coefficient	Total	Comments
1	A X	Enter in working trot Halt, salute, proceed at working trot	10				
2	C E	Track left Circle left 20 metres	10				
3	Between K & A	Working trot sitting	10				
4	Between A & F	Working canter left leg	10		2		
5	B	Circle left 20 metres On returning to B working trot	10				
6	C HXF	Medium walk Change rein free walk on a long rein	10		2		
7	A E	Working trot Circle right 20 metres	10				
8	Between H & C	Working trot sitting	10				
9	Between C & M	Working canter right leg	10		2		
10	B	Circle right 20 metres On returning to B working trot	10				
11	A G	Turn up centre line Halt, salute	10				
		Leave the arena at a free walk on a long rein at A					
Collective marks							
Paces of the horse			10		2		
Impulsion, relaxation, engagement			10		2		
Submission and obedience			10		2		
Rider's position and effectiveness of the aids			10		2		
Total marks			230				

Appendix 3: Example show program

Ring 2 – GALLOWAYS. Commencing 9:00am   Judge: Mr John Brown

1   Smartest on parade 12 yrs & under 14 yrs
2   Smartest on parade 14 yrs & under 16 yrs
3   Smartest on parade 16 yrs & under 18 yrs
4   Led Galloway over 14hh n/e 14.2hh
5   Led Galloway over 14.2hh n/e 15hh
Champion & Reserve Champion Led Galloway classes 4 & 5

6   Novice rider 12 yrs & under 18 yrs
7   Rider 12 yrs & under 14 yrs
8   Rider 14 yrs & under 16 yrs
9   Rider 16 yrs & under 18 yrs
Champion & Reserve Champion Intermediate rider classes 6–9

10 Child's Galloway, must be ridden by a child 14 yrs and under
11 Pleasure Galloway, must be ridden in snaffle bit, no whips or spurs
12 Novice ridden Galloway 14hh n/e 15hh
13 Ridden Galloway 14hh n/e 14.2hh
14 Ridden Galloway 14.2hh n/e 15hh
Champion & Reserve Champion Ridden Galloway classes 12–14

Further reading and website links

Bartle, Christopher & Newsum, Gillian (2004). *Training the sport horse.* JA Allen: London.

British Horse Society (2001). *The BHS manual of equitation.* Kenilworth Press: Buckingham, UK.

German National Equestrian Federation (2004). *The principles of riding.* Kenilworth Press: Buckingham, UK.

Kidd, Jane (2007). *To be a dressage rider.* The Pony Club: Warwickshire, UK.

Mairinger, Franz (1996). *Horses are made to be horses.* Rigby: Adelaide.

McKeown, Brian (2003). *Enter at A, laughing.* Half halt Press: Boonsboro, MD. (For the non-riding spouse).

McLean, Andrew (2003). *The truth about horses. A guide to understanding and training your horse.* Viking Press: Melbourne.

Richter, Judy (2003). *Riding for kids.* Storey Books: North Adams, MA.

Roberts, Tom (1982). *Horse control – the rider.* TA & PR Roberts.

Ross, Eleanor (1992). *School exercises for flatwork and jumping.* Kenilworth Press: Shrewsbury, UK.

Stockdale, Tim & Draper, Judith (2006). *A young person's guide to show jumping.* The Pony Club: Warwickshire, UK.

Troup, Melissa (2006). *Everyday jumping for riders and instructors.* Kenilworth Press: Shrewsbury, UK.

Website links

Equestrian Federation of Australia

www.efanational.com (national)

www.vic.equestrian.org.au (Vic.)

www.qld.equestrian.org.au (Qld)

www.sa.equestrian.org.au (SA)

www.efansw.com.au (NSW)

www.wa.equestrian.org.au (WA)

Pony club associations
www.ponyclubvic.org.au (Vic.)
www.ponyclub-australia.org (national)
www.pcaq.asn.au (Qld)
www.pcansw.org.au (NSW)
www.ponyclub.asn.au (SA)
www.pcat.org.au (Tas.)
www.pcawa.com (WA)

Riding club associations
www.hrcav.com.au (Horse Riding Club Association of Victoria)

Various
www.malbyrne.com.au (master saddler)
www.gillian-rolton.com (Gillian Rolton)
www.cyberhorse.net.au/tve (equestrian website)
www.eques.com.au (equestrian website)
www.horsedeals.com.au (horse trading magazine website)
www.horsemagazine.com (horse magazine website)
www.horsehive.com (equestrian website)
www.eqlife.com.au (equestrian magazine website)

Index